LORD RADSTOCK of MAYFIELD

LORD RADSTOCK of MAYFIELD

by

David Fountain

MAYFLOWER CHRISTIAN BOOKS

The Publishing Branch of
MAYFLOWER CHRISTIAN BOOKSHOPS CHARITABLE TRUST
114, Spring Road, Sholing, Southampton, Hants.

Copyright © 1984 Mayflower Christian Books

ISBN 0 907821 03 0

Cover Design by Ruth Goodridge

Typeset by Print Co-ordination, Macclesfield, Cheshire

Printed by
Deslith (Print & Design) Ltd., 20 City Commerce Centre, Marsh Lane, Southampton SO1 1EW

Contents

Foreword

Author's Preface

1 — Background and Early Life 1

2 — Beginnings of Christian Service 5

3 — Russia 13

4 — Russia (continued) 29

5 — Further Travels 43

6 — Southampton and Mayfield 53

7 — Closing Days 65

Appendix: Letters 75

References 83

About the Author

David Fountain was educated at Dulwich College and studied history at St. Peter's Hall, Oxford, where he obtained his M.A. He has been pastor of Spring Road Evangelical Church, Sholing, Southampton, since 1955. He has written a number of books on historical themes including:-

1970:   The Mayflower Pilgrims and their Pastor (350th Anniversary)

1974:   Isaac Watts Remembered (300th Anniversary of his birth)

1984:   John Wycliffe The Dawn of the Reformation (600th Anniversary of his death)

Other Mayflower publications include:-

A Stone Made Smooth
                    — *Autobiography of Wong Ming-Dao*

Spiritual Food
                    — *Selected Writings of Wong Ming-Dao*

A Light Shines in Poland

Foreword

One of the most remarkable transformations in the spiritual life of any nation of which we have record is that which took place in England during the course of the nineteenth century. A society rough, disorderly, often gin soaked and violent at the poorer levels; equally often morally corrupt, venal and ruthless in its richer manifestations, became by the end of the century one in which a quite astonishing change could be observed. Terrible blemishes of poverty and of excess doubtless remained: but an extraordinary flowering of self-discipline and moral zeal had, broadly, turned the least law abiding of the great nations into a society famed for civil order, and had done it on the basis of a flowering of Christian belief and morality perhaps unparalleled in modern times. Central to this rebirth (the benefits of which are only now, a century later sadly beginning to ebb away) was the extraordinary power of the evangelical revival, manifesting itself not only in a reaffirmation of Christianity at home and abroad, but in practical work for the poor, in campaigns against alcohol and prostitution, for prison reform, housing for the poor, and many other admirable causes. My family mirrors this transformation in microcosm. In its Radstock branch it produced a whole family which embodied the practical force of the evangelical upsurge of energy, with Granville Waldegrave, 3rd Baron Radstock, as its most remarkable member. In the senior branch, from which I am descended, Regency 'black sheep' worthy to be the villains of Dickens or Thackeray, were succeeded in mid-century by decent and public spirited men and women strongly tinged with evangelical fervour. I therefore think this biography, in recounting the story of a remarkable Christian, tells also an important part of the story of our nation, and indeed of the evangelical Englishmen who carried Christianity far and wide beyond our shores.

William Waldegrave

Author's Preface

For many years I have wanted to write a life of the late Lord Radstock (the 3rd Baron), whose estate I can see from my study. I learned a great deal about him from the late Mrs. Eva McGregor, who knew him personally and looked after his grandchildren at Mayfield House. She was an invaluable source of information. I had the further privilege of receiving Radstock's own Bible (which is illustrated in the book), one of his chairs (which is in my study), together with other mementos. Another very useful source of information is Mrs. Jean Weller. Her husband was Lord Radstock's valet. He shared with her important details about his Lordship, which she remembered.

Last year I wrote to the Hon. William Waldegrave, MP., because his name suggested that he was related to Radstock (Waldegrave being the family name). When he wrote back last year he confirmed that there was, indeed, a connection: the first Lord Radstock was the younger brother of the 6th Earl Waldegrave, from whom he was descended. I was delighted when he agreed to write a Foreword to the book. He, helpfully, passed on the name and address of Lady Hersey Goring, wife of Radstock's grandson, John, who died during the Second World War. She was able to supply me with obituary notices, photographs and letters. These letters included some from the Queens of Sweden and Denmark, which are included in the book. This was tremendously helpful.

While I was proceeding with the book in the Autumn of '87, I discovered that the Radstock estate was sold to the Southampton Corporation on the death of the 4th Baron in 1937, and in 1938 it became a public park. This was opened on the 23rd June of that year by the Mayor. I was amazed that, in God's providence, the book should be out just in time for the Jubilee of the opening of Mayfield Park to the public. The park staff have been very interested in the celebrations, and the City Archivist, Sheila Thompson, who has been a great help, found a brief film of the opening itself 50 years ago. Jill Neil, of the City Museums, and Ian Abrahams of the Mayfield Park staff, have been particularly helpful. Others have also been of great assistance. These include Myna Trustram of Tudor House, Jean Chenery, Ian Chenery, Ruth Goodridge, Andrew Fountain and Michael Underwood, who have assisted in a variety of ways.

I have wanted to write about Lord Radstock, not only because he lived so near my home but because he was such a remarkable man. Very few know much about him and, of those who do, scarcely any have been aware of the extraordinary effect of his evangelistic work in Russia. Some years ago I was told in a letter about a book written by Professor Edmund Heier, "Religious Schism in the Russian Aristocracy 1860-1900 - Radstockism and Pashkovism" (published by Martinus Nijhoff). I simply put the letter away in the drawer, that I kept for the information I was accumulating about Lord Radstock, until I had time to undertake the work. When I eventually obtained this book I was absolutely astonished. Professor Heier has produced an amazing record of Radstock's achievements and the religious awakening in Russia. The documentation is so thorough that none would doubt the authenticity and reliability of his thesis. I want to express my deepest gratitude to Professor Heier, who has kindly allowed me to make use of his work. Copies of the publication are available from "Mayflower Christian Books".

Sadly Mayfield Home has gone, but photographs remain. This book contains the best of them, but also a brief record of the man who lived there, with his family. His life shines out as example of the godliness and dedication to the cause of Christ. How we need such examples in these days.

Chapter 1.
Background and Early Life

Tributes.

When Lord Radstock died on 8th December, 1913, many tributes were paid to him from public figures at home and abroad. It became clear to those who did not know him that the world had lost a truly outstanding man. "The Times" reported that, "In the 3rd Baron Radstock there has passed away an altogether exceptional man whose career has been as remarkable as it is, to the present generation at least, unknown. In the modern world, the figure of an English nobleman who, abandoning the normal interests and occupations of his class, devotes his life to missionary enterprise... is an unusual if not unique phenomenon". Such words well sum up the outstanding career of the subject of our biography. Great numbers, in many countries, benefited from his many activities, not least the poor of the East End of London. This came out in the many letters of appreciation received by the family.

What remains as an enduring monument to his missionary work is the result of his labours in Russia. He has no heirs to carry on his title, but he has many spiritual heirs in the Soviet Union. They bear his likeness in that they share his dedication to the cause of Christ. The work he undertook in St. Petersburg (Leningrad), and the success of his activities, are little known in this country. It forms one of the most amazing chapters in church history, through God's grace. A great spiritual awakening began through what he did, and spread across the entire breadth of that vast country. Today, there are thousands of churches that owe their spiritual foundation to a large degree to Radstock himself. It is not by chance that his portrait hangs today in one of the Baptist churches at Leningrad. But, while the Baptists of Russia today trace their spiritual ancestry to Radstock among others, Radstock could trace his own ancestry back to very early times.

Ancestry.

The name of Waldegrave (the family name) can be honourably traced right back to before William the Conqueror. Radstock's grandfather, the first Baron, was Admiral the Honourable William Waldegrave, C.B.C., second son of the 3rd Earl Waldegrave. The Admiral was a forceful and dominant man and, at the same time, God-fearing and most generous. These characteristics bear a striking resemblance to those of his grandson. His father, the 2nd Baron Radstock, was a Vice-Admiral, and married Esther Caroline, youngest daughter of John Puget, a Director of the Bank of England. She was descended from an old Huguenot family. Her mother had been widowed early and, having inherited great wealth, she gave to many charities. These included Indian and Siberian missions, French and German Protestant causes, and the poor of London and Ireland. It is said that she would spend nights talking to condemned criminals, and would travel at great personal discomfort to help the suffering. We again see characteristics that were later to appear in her grandson.

Early Life.

Granville Augustus William Waldegrave, the subject of our biography, was born on 2nd April, 1833. His mother ensured he was given a sound education, not only naturally, but also spiritually. She laid in him a Scriptural foundation at an early age that was to bear fruit in later years. On one occasion, as a little boy, he drew her attention to a verse of Scripture with great pleasure. "Such a pretty verse I have found: 'The righteous shall hold on his way, and he that hath clean hands shall wax stronger and stronger'."

He had an impetuous nature. As a child, he would run at great speed and fall headlong, but would get up and carry on. He imagined he was some great prince with boundless energy, not thinking of himself but of what he might achieve. Thus, the behaviour of the boy in his physical activity seems to tell us how he was to grow up. It was said of him after he died, by "The Times", that he "was a man of enormous energy and determination, who followed what he conceived to be the right path without the slightest regard for the consequences"; but he was yet to devote his energy to the Kingdom of God.

He went to Harrow School. While he was there he lived without serious thought of God. For him it would be enough to maintain a nominal profession of Christianity. This, he felt, would secure his salvation, but in his heart he knew that all was not right. After an accident, someone challenged him as to what would have happened to him if he had died. He didn't know because he knew there was something basically wrong with his life. His mother's influence had made its mark. He went up to Oxford and, at Balliol College, took a double second in Modern History and Physical Science. He rowed for the college and developed an interest in music, to which he was devoted. He led an active life typical of a young man with all his advantages.

Conversion.

He pursued the pleasures of this world with great energy, imagining he could forget about the next—but he was soon to face another world. Going to the Crimea as an Army officer he witnessed the horrors of the battlefield. The conditions there have become notorious through Florence Nightingale's work. Soon, he was to become a victim, and was struck down with fever. He was given up by the doctors. "My last hour has come", he said to himself, "and I am not ready." But he knew the way of salvation; the instruction and prayers of his mother were not in vain. His cry for deliverance and salvation was heard. When he recovered it was to everyone's surprise; but far greater was the surprise of those who found that he had become a new man!

He returned to London to begin the great work that God had given him to do. He had experienced personal salvation through the Lord Jesus Christ when he became aware of his need. This experience could not be inherited—it was by grace alone. He had humbled himself and had been brought to see the One of whom his mother had frequently told him. He was a man exceptionally endowed with great natural gifts, and was soon to hold a position that gave him contacts with the very highest in society. God had prepared his servant for a great life work.

Chapter 2.
Beginnings of Christian Service

Young Waldegrave was impetuous by nature and full of energy, but it was only by stages that he gave himself fully to Christian service. It was several years before he reached the intensity of activity which he kept up throughout the rest of his life.

A Turning Point.

When he returned to London from the Crimea it was the beginning of another Society season. To begin with, he followed the customary pattern of balls, dinners and entertainments in the company of his Belgravia friends. However, on one occasion a well-known barrister challenged him by asking him what he was doing for Christ, his new Master. After being convicted in this way he began to do some hospital visitation and, rather unwillingly, went to the Middlesex Hospital to read to the sick and dying.

An incident took place at this time which was to have a profound effect on young Waldegrave. A young man from the Philippines was brought in as a patient. He was suffering from a terrible cancer that was eating away his face. He was bitter and resentful, but Waldegrave, who knew no Spanish, was determined to do something for this wretched individual. He decided to read a Spanish New Testament, and watched the expression on the listener's face as he found that he could be understood. He read such passages as Ephesians 2:4-9: "God, who is rich in mercy, for His great love wherewith He loved us, even when we were dead in sins, hath quickened us together with Christ... For by grace are ye saved through faith; and that not of yourselves: it is the gift of God"; and John 3:16: "For God so loved the world that He gave His only begotten Son, that whosoever believeth in Him should not perish but have everlasting life".

He read such passages over and over again for several weeks. A profound change came over the man. The nurses spoke of what had happened. Somebody visited him who could speak Spanish and discovered he had come to an experience of peace in the Lord Jesus Christ. The very next day he died. This was the first person who had come to an experience of the living God through Waldegrave. He would never forget it, and it was to be repeated for the rest of his life. Clearly, it was not Waldegrave's persuasiveness that was the cause of the change, but simply the Word of God, and Waldegrave would have remembered that. He learned to place his confidence in the Gospel message, and that confidence increased and proved well-founded.

He Inherits the Title.

When he was only twenty-three he succeeded to the title and became the 3rd Baron Radstock. Two years later he married Susan, daughter of John Hales Calcraft, M.P. of Rempstone, Dorset, and of Caroline his wife, daughter of the 5th Duke of Manchester. She was very beautiful and gracious. Dr. David Livingstone thought very highly of her: "I have seen Lady Radstock. She is as good as she is beautiful".

Christian Service.

In his mid-twenties Radstock had great advantages and few limitations. He had no need to work, such were his private means. His health was excellent, his constitution strong, and his talents many. He could, at this point, have easily pursued a political career as he had a particular talent for diplomacy. He was approached by a well-known peer who wanted to propose him for election as an Irish representative peer. He received the suggestion kindly, but said straight away, "Whom could I represent? I could never stand for anyone but myself". He said later, "I am convinced that, even if I had every possible success, I should never have known one tenth of the happiness which I have had in God's service, even in this world." He gave up much, but he received far more. He once said of those who sought pleasure in this life only, "Oh, what they are losing!".

He and his wife settled down in Bryanston Square, and such was his popularity that they had hundreds of invitations to dinner every year. However, as his spiritual convictions strengthened, he became more determined to witness for his new Master, and so the invitations declined. He saw how much emptiness and hypocrisy lay behind Society life, and could not bear to spend time and energy merely socialising. Consequently, whenever he received an invitation to a social gathering, he sought the same kind of guidance he would need before speaking at a Christian meeting. In his own words, "Every detail, while it is the fruit of the past, is a seed of the future. One seed dropped by a bird in a new land often leads to the introduction of a totally different kind of vegetation which, in its turn, acts on the insect life, which again reacts on the animal, and so on human life and destiny". This was to prove exactly the case with contacts which eventually led him to his greatest work in Russia, as we shall see later.

Life in London.

Lady Buxton gives us a glimpse of this period of their life together in their London home: "...they both were a good deal in society, where he was always trying to do his Master's work in a quiet and unobtrusive way. I remember about that time, when he was taking me down to dinner one evening in a friend's house, how he asked me whether I had been able to do any work for the Master the last time I had dined out: I felt reproved."

"I used frequently to go to their house on Saturday evenings in Bryanston Square where, after his Saturday night's (military) drill, he and Lady Radstock used to have small Bible readings. Amongst others whom I met at these Bible readings were Lord Charles Russell, Lord Congleton, Lord Reay, and others, and we used to sit round the table and talk over the passage read. I often think of some of the original and evidently heartfelt comments that he used to make—one especially: he was speaking of the passage Matthew 11:28,29, and he drew our attention to the two 'rests' there spoken of. The rest of forgiveness, 'Come unto me and I will give you rest', and the further rest of submission of the will, 'Take my yoke upon you... and ye shall find rest unto your souls'. He said that some Christians had the first rest without the second and the second was the one we all ought to aim at and pray for through life." The 'rest' he referred to, which is the privilege of those who submit to the will of their Master, became for him an on-going experience. As Lady Buxton continued: "He certainly practised what he preached more than any one I can remember. I used to observe how, no doubt in order to give more away, they parted at that time with jewels, china and carriage one after another".

Sacrifice.

He began to make sacrifices early in his life as a Christian, but a moment of special significance was the occasion when he gave up his work with the West Middlesex Volunteers. He recruited and trained his own battalion. "Radstock's Battalion" became a familiar sight in Hyde Park, where he led them on his grey charger. He was so skilful as an officer that his Commander-in-Chief, the Duke of Cambridge, said there was hardly an officer in the army who could vie with him in getting 20,000 men in and out of Hyde Park!

This work had taken a tremendous amount of time, energy and resources, and it was a sacrifice he was no longer willing to make. It meant the loss of many contacts, but led to others being opened up. It was when he heard Hudson Taylor, the great missionary to China, speak that he realised that there must be a great change in his life. Hudson Taylor had done so much with so little initial help from those at home and Radstock was troubled in his conscience.

Call to Service.

It was at this time that he felt the call to devote his whole life to the preaching of the Gospel. Giving up the command of his battalion would free him to respond to invitations to speak at Christian meetings. He was soon in demand, and found himself taking a series of meetings at

Weston-super-Mare. These proved to be very productive, particularly in the case of the conversion of a German named Dr. Baedeker. He was persuaded to go to one of the meetings, which were attended by great numbers. On the second occasion, after a private chat with Radstock, he came to a living faith in Christ: "I went in a proud German infidel, and came out a humble, believing disciple of the Lord Jesus Christ. Praise God!". This was the very man who went to Russia eight years later. He was introduced by Radstock to those in high society who had been converted through him. By this means Baedeker was able to engage in his great work of visiting prisons from one end of Siberia to the other.

Travels Abroad.

Radstock did not limit his preaching to England, but visited many European countries as well as visiting India later in his life. In 1867, he was invited to speak in Holland, where there was a great response. He also did much good by his personal witness, and just such an example is given by someone who was living at the Hague at the time: "I remember one day, while dining out with him, the young people were making arrangements for some Sunday amusement, when one turned to him saying, 'I suppose you think this very wrong?' 'Well', he answered, 'we are all on a voyage; if on our boat we each have the right pilot at the helm, we can't go wrong'. And then and there, at table, he gave the most direct, glorious Gospel message, lifting up Christ in all His beauty and fullness… The chief work in Holland was amongst the upper classes, and these were helped and encouraged to evangelise throughout the country".

Lady Radstock.

Some may wonder how his wife, Lady Susan, felt about Radstock's activities. It could mean long periods of absence from home, though he would take her with him on occasions. A letter from a friend to Lord Radstock's daughter gives us some idea of the impression her mother made on those who knew her: "I was a very great deal at your house in Bryanston Square when you were all tiny children. My mother was a very dear friend of yours, and I used to go with her to their evening meetings, sometimes for Bible readings, though I remember some missionary meetings (China Inland Mission) and one or two prophetical ones... I vaguely realised that the life in your house was different from any other life I had ever known, but it was not till some years later that I understood what it all meant. I was very timid and shy, and I don't think I ever talked to your father. To tell the honest truth I was rather afraid of him. But I may say this from my heart, I did love your mother deeply, surely the most lovable and saintly woman I ever knew... I spent my time with her, and the remembrance of her saintly beautiful life has lived with me ever since. I have a strong feeling that married women ought to leave most outside work to their unmarried sisters, and I am sure your mother felt this. She acted as if she did. So, to sum it all up, the impression on me as I look back on both their lives is, that a very great measure of your father's wonderful success in influencing people's lives was due to his beautiful saintly wife, who I know was following him with her loving interest and prayers whenever and wherever he was preaching..."

It would take up many pages to do justice to Radstock's many and varied activities because this itinerant peer went to so many countries and did such a remarkable work. However, we must give special attention to his work in Russia, as this has left the greatest mark. In other countries his activities were part of a wider movement that was affecting a great many people at this time. His own individual contribution was lost amidst such activity. In Russia we can see what he was able to achieve on his own, by the grace of God. We see here a unique work: a single individual, totally committed to the advance of the Kingdom of God, was used in a way that has few parallels in history.

Chapter 3.
Russia

Radstock is best remembered for the great work he accomplished in Russia. His place in the spiritual history of that country is unique.

St. Petersburg.

He appeared in St. Petersburg (Leningrad) at a time when the Established Church was at its lowest ebb. At the same time, there was a hunger for better things. It is worthy of note that great work of preparation had been going on for some years. At the same time Radstock himself was also being prepared, as we shall see later. He was used to initiate a religious awakening that reached staggering proportions. His links with Russia are familiar to many, but the strength of the spiritual awakening he initiated is largely unknown.

Many such movements are very hard to assess because of an absence of solid evidence and a tendency to exaggerate results. Radstock's work, however, has been painstakingly documented. In 1970, Martinus Nijhoff (The Hague), published *Religious Schism in the Russian Aristocracy 1860-1900 RADSTOCKISM AND PASHKOVISM* by

Edmund Heier. Professor Heier is extremely well-qualified, and the bibliography reveals the massive research that has gone into this book. The enormous number of primary sources gives the reader complete confidence in the scholarship of the author. According to Professor Heier, "The religious movement initiated by the English Lord Radstock in the 1870's... reached a staggering growth within the next few decades." Very few are aware of the extent of this spiritual awakening.

The movement deserves our special attention, not only for its own sake but because it highlights the unique character of Lord Radstock. In St. Petersburg he was the sole instrument, to begin with. Those who followed him copied his example so that he put his stamp on the whole revival. It is clear in Scripture and in church history that God uses examples. In Russia, Radstock's example and experience were fully exposed and followed, in an enormous number of cases, by both great and small—by the grace of God.

Professor Heier makes this point: "Though active... in his native England, in France, Holland, Switzerland, and in India, his greatest imprint was made in Russia during the 1870's. It was there that the name Radstock became known in every corner of the country and where the new religious teaching gave rise to ardent discussions. Even those who could not pronounce his name properly discussed his teachings..."[1] There was nothing "new" about Radstock's "religious teaching", but it was certainly new to his hearers, who were unaccustomed to the simple message of the grace of God.

Preparation.

Before he arrived in St. Petersburg in the Spring of 1874 he had been prepared in his own experience. Russian Society had also been prepared. A letter from a friend to his biographer, Mrs. Trotter, gives us a very clear insight into the preparation he underwent before he got there. She wrote, "I was taught by his holy consistent life and simple waiting upon God for guidance in the least as well as in the greatest matters, more even than by his words. He was then thinking of banding together young Christians whose knowledge of continental languages would enable them to go abroad and win souls to Christ from the higher circles of society. Especially in Russia did he seek an opening for such work for himself, and he told me that for ten years he had waited for such a door to open to him, but that hitherto the door had only been ajar, so he was then educating his eldest daughter to go to Russia in his stead. Then he said to me 'Never push open a door ajar; God says, "I have set before thee an open door," when He means us to go forward; but He sometimes lets our faith be tried by doors ajar that we may wait to see if He means them to be opened to us.' When we met a year or two later at Bonchurch, Isle of Wight, Lord Radstock told me how God had taken his daughter Home, but had opened the way wide for him to go himself to Russia and carry on the work there, in which later he was so greatly blessed, thus giving to me a lesson never to be forgotten."

With him, one great principle of guidance was to examine one's motives very carefully. Clearly, he had a very great desire to preach the Gospel to those in Russia, and this persisted with him for some years until he was able to go himself. Russia was on his heart to the very end of his life. It is important to realise that he did not need to speak Russian in order to preach to the upper classes (though he did learn to speak it to some degree). He was able to preach in French because it was fashionable in High Society to converse in French, and that language was well-known in St. Petersburg.

Providence.

To Radstock, the Providence of God was all-important. He recognised that the smallest events could lead to great things. "The tsetse fly in South Africa has been one of the most potent factors in the social, commercial and military affairs of that continent. Was the first tsetse an unimportant personage?" In keeping with such convictions, he was to experience an unexpected series of events that led to his invitation to Russia. He was in Paris, and a Russian diplomat who knew him tried in vain to obtain for him an interview with a certain Grand Duchess. However, Radstock was unexpectedly called upon to visit a Princess. He arrived early, having taken a cab (contrary to his custom!) as he was particularly tired from walking all day in the heat.

No sooner had he arrived than the Duchess herself arrived unexpectedly and, not seeing Radstock, announced that she was going to spend the evening there. She ended up talking to Radstock with great earnestness. Before her return to Russia she talked with him for five hours, and invited him to her native country. He also had an invitation from Madam Chertkova, wife of the General Adjutant to the Czar, and mother of one of Tolstoy's closest associates. She had met him in Switzerland, and had been especially comforted by him after the death of her two sons. When he arrived in St. Petersburg during the 'Holy Week' of the Spring of 1874, he was thus fully prepared—but so were those to whom he was to speak, and consequently the response was immediate. Many others who were to be influenced by his converts were likewise prepared and their response was identical.

Religion in Russia.

The spiritual condition of the Orthodox (Established) Church in Russia in the 1870's bears some resemblance to that of the Church of England in the 1730's, before the Methodist Awakening. The Orthodox Church had become thoroughly worldly and had almost lost all respect among the populace. However, there had been a very real spiritual work accomplished earlier in the century which had left its mark, and there was a stirring among those who were concerned about the state of affairs. Besides this, there were Nonconformists who kept the bright light of the Gospel shining in parts of the Empire.

Professor Heier makes a comparison between Radstock and Wesley, and the parallel holds good in a number of ways. "His 'religious activity' was evangelical, or of the 'Low Church' variety. Its starting-point may be linked with Wesley and his successors in early Methodism. What he offered was a spiritual faith in opposition to the worldliness of the Established Church."[2] He ministered to those within the Established Church in Russia, and the movement began within that body, as was the case with Methodism in England. The Church of England of the 18th century, however, unlike the Russian Orthodox Church, derived from the Reformation. Radstock, however, saw Orthodoxy as a transitional state of Christianity, and was very optimistic because of the numbers that were seeking Christ. This explains, in part, why the movement grew up within the Established Church, and not outside it. It touched the highest in the land, and reached vast numbers of the common people, but this aroused hostility from the ecclesiastical authorities. Persecution drove people out of the Established Church, as was the case in England.

Nevertheless, they strengthened the ranks of Nonconformity that had been supporting them, as happened, too, in England.

Social Movement.

Previous to Radstock's arrival in St. Petersburg there had been a prolonged conflict between the old conservatism and a new liberalism in Russia. "Reform and liberalism alternated with Nihilism and terrorism; various social movements with revolutionary activities and the spread of religious nonconformity were met with reaction, repression, and persecution".[3] There was a great concern to build a new society, and many of the nobility felt guilty because of the way they had treated the peasants, but the Government was suspicious of any that challenged the status quo, and Nihilism was clearly dangerous. This was popular among the youth of the 1860's and 1870's, and was defined as "a negative attitude towards existing convention, social, political and religious institutions". According to Heier, they "rejected absolute values, and believed only in the scientific for the solution of all problems".[4]

It was not difficult to find good reasons to resist change, but change had to come, and this was a constant problem. It is amazing how history repeats itself! The failure of the movement for change led to a disillusionment and a feeling of hopelessness. The literature of the time reflected this pessimism. In the religious sphere, disillusionment with the Established Church led to the growth of Nonconformity. As the Church was subservient to the State it was subject to the hostility felt against the State, and those who opposed the Church were persecuted as being unpatriotic. "The official church, through its intimate connection with the State, stood as the adversary of progress",

Heier explains.[5] Atheism was spreading among the upper classes, and apathy had a general hold.

Spiritual Preparation.

While the great masses of the people were left to grope in the dark, there was a clear witness to the faith in many places among the sects. These had been nurtured by the distribution of the Scriptures earlier in the century. During the reign of Czar Alexander I, nearly one million Bibles, in about thirty languages spoken in the Empire, were circulated. This was done through the 289 Auxiliaries of the Bible Society set up by Prince Galitsin in 1814, with the support of Czar Alexander I himself. The Prince had earlier been instrumental in bringing the Czar to seek and find Christ. The British and Foreign Bible Society gave great assistance here. Even after the Russian Bible Society was dissolved by Czar Nicholas I, it did a considerable amount of work in Russia through a Scotsman, Melville. He distributed Bibles among the non-Orthodox population.

It was inevitable that this great work had its effect. Heier points out that, "the history of the Russian Bible translation is closely linked with the religious revival of the 1870's. The New and the Old Testaments were published for the first time officially in the Russian vernacular by the Holy Synod between 1867-76 and thus were made accessible to the literate Russian. This publication no doubt… encouraged its interpretation independently of the doctrines of the church. This contributed to creating an atmosphere favourable to Lord Radstock's teaching".[6] It led to greater attention being paid to the Bible, and Prayer Meetings and Bible Studies were arranged in private houses. Thus the way was prepared, in the sovereignty of God, for the visit of Lord Radstock; but there was another factor of equal importance.

Count Korff.

The activities of Count Korff, Lord Chamberlain at the Czar's court, must be mentioned here, for they are as important as they are extraordinary. He had been at the World Exhibition in Paris in 1867, and there, coming across the stand of the British and Foreign Bible Society, he conversed with one of the attendants. As a result of this, to his complete amazement, he received three thousand copies of St. John's Gospel when he returned home, and was asked to distribute them for the Bible Society. He was horrified, but felt that the Holy Synod would relieve him from his embarrassment by prohibiting it—but they gave him permission! Korff had not yet been converted: this was to await Radstock's arrival; but he was being prepared, and was preparing others. The Bible Society, being encouraged by his assistance, asked him to distribute complete Bibles! He did this, and circulated no less than 62,000 copies in the year 1870.

Fourteen years later he was to be exiled for doing the very same thing when the ecclesiastical authorities realised that this encouraged the growth of Dissenters within the Empire. Count Korff was to become a key figure in the movement as he was "a confidante of almost every member of the Royal Family. He listened one evening to a talk in which Radstock explained the sacrificial death of Christ, and he came to see that his own sins were borne away on the cross".[7]

Revival.

Radstock had waited ten years to visit Russia. When the time had come, he and those he was to address were prepared. Princess Catherine Galitsin, granddaughter of the man who was President of the Russian Bible Society, described what happened. "By Heaven's power all doors were thrown open to him—halls, chapels and private houses; whole crowds pressed in to hear the glad tidings. It was just after a week of religious rites that I went to see my cousin, Princess Leiven. There I met Lord Radstock, who had just arrived in St. Petersburg."[8] Peter Masters goes on, "Princess Catherine derived great pleasure from the pomp and splendour of the Russian Orthodox church ritual, and she told the English lord about the emotions it stirred within her. But Radstock was not prepared to leave her trusting the shallow, emotional feelings drawn from ritualistic religion. He wanted her to know Christ, and told her how she could."[9]

She "was thrown into a quandary. Had she been worshipping a mere shadow all her life? Could God be known? She began to attend every possible meeting which Lord Radstock held. 'At length,' she wrote, 'after a most blessed sermon, I remained for a private conversation and there we both knelt in prayer before the One who became my Saviour for ever.' Princess Natalie Leiven of St. Petersburg soon followed her cousin in going to Christ for forgiveness of sins and an experience of new life. Day after day Radstock found himself visiting the lofty, extravagant drawing rooms of St Petersburg, pressing the aristocracy to see their need of Christ. Night after night he would be found preaching through an interpreter to crowded halls. His conversations with the nobility were always in French, which was then spoken by all well-placed members of Russian society.

Almost at once a fashionable St. Petersburg newspaper was protesting at the alarming spread of Protestantism. Under the headline: 'A new apostle in the high society' it described the great following Lord Radstock had attracted, complaining bitterly that royal ladies sent him dozens of invitations to hold meetings in their homes. Radstock himself was filled with amazement by the effects of his work. 'When I started,' he said, 'several of my Russian friends thought I had better not go. I was able to have six or seven public meetings a week in French or English, but the greatest part of my time (in all: eight to fourteen hours a day) was occupied in visits to private houses'."[10]

It is clear that an enormous number of people gathered to hear Radstock, many of whom were drawn from the aristocracy. The question naturally arises, was this just another religious craze? In the midst of the disillusionment with the Orthodox Church, people were like the Athenians—looking for anything new, and were particularly open to ideas coming from the West. It was indeed something unusual for them to hear an English lord, who had come to preach to them in French. While it is true that there was novelty, there was little else that was attractive.

A novel written at this time gives an interesting description of Radstock himself: "The new arrival seems to be about fifty years old or more. He was dressed in a simple grey overcoat, and nothing in his manner reminded one of a preacher. Large and tall, he was an imposing figure. A square forehead and bald head, framed with a crown of wispy blond hair, short, red side-whiskers, a clear and benevolent look, an almost habitual smile illuminated his face; such was the 'lord apostle', as his detractors called him". Prince Mechtchersky, the famous satirical writer, endeavoured to ridicule the whole movement in his novel, "Lord Apostel", but nothing could stop it growing.

The Movement Spreads.

The mansions of Princesses Leiven and Gagarin, Counts Korff and Brobinsky, and especially the homes of Col. Pashkof, became permanent meeting places. Radstock was occupied almost non-stop, speaking to both congregations and individuals. "The Times", in the obituary article on Radstock, referred to the words of M. Leroy-Beaulieu. He said that at the end of the reign of Alexander II the drawing-rooms of St. Petersburg contained many "spirits famishing for truth and disgusted with the insipidity of the traditional bakemeats served by the official clergy in their heavy plates of gold". To appeal to exalted personages in these circles no ordinary preacher was required. To this blasé society "the Word of God was brought by an English Lord". This "high-class missionary", continued the French historian, "quickly became fashionable. His familiar homilies competed with the spiritualistic seances which were much in vogue at the same time. He preached at evening parties or at 5 o'clock tea, as did the popular prophets round the samovar in the taverns. It was generally in French that Lord Radstock instructed the Russian ladies. Sceptics had a fine opportunity for making fun of the apostle-lord, but the evangelic seed sprang up none the less from falling on drawing-room carpets."

Radstock's Preaching.

It was a mystery to many how services that lacked the splendour of the Orthodox Church could attract so many. He would begin with a silent prayer for guidance, then read the Scriptures and follow with an exposition of the passage read. The service would last for an hour. His central theme was the fundamentals of the Gospel, namely that salvation comes through faith in the Lord Jesus Christ, who died as an atonement on the cross, and that we can know that we have been forgiven. He would conclude with a prayer and a hymn. He also invited all those who wanted to "find Christ" to call on him later, if they so desired. Meetings were conducted "in a conversational tone, almost a whisper, without emotion or eloquence, but with a deep conviction".[11] In his personal interviews he made his position clear. He only recognised baptism and the Lord's Supper as ordinances, and was content to declare himself as a member of the church of Christ "in general", rather than any individual denomination.

He particularly emphasised the Doctrine of Justification by Faith, as Luther expounded it from Romans. Good works were of no value in securing salvation. We were

incapable of doing anything to merit forgiveness: salvation was a free gift, but good works were the expression of gratitude for that free gift and the proof that we had received it. Orthodox priests were alarmed, and he was often misrepresented. Radstock simply used Scripture to prove that good works were the result of salvation, not the grounds of it. We were saved by what Christ had done, and by nothing else. He avoided any subject, either religious or political, that would detract from the simple theme of the Gospel.

The Extent of the Revival.

The success of his mission was enormous, as Heier records: "A correspondent for the Orthodox Church-Public Messenger records in 1874 that after attending a meeting he is unable to state the reason for the impressions made upon him by the speaker's discourse. Both friend and foe admit that there was certainly nothing in himself to account for the effect which his preaching produced. Yet his evangelical message, without profundity of thought, without theology and precise explanations, and in faulty French, was eagerly welcomed by the 'Orthodox barons, princes, counts, and generals' as a fresh revelation of Christian truth. In the words of a Russian general 'he (Radstock) was but the telegraph wire; through him came the spark from on high' at the moment of deepest spiritual frustration. But apart from this, it was the simplicity of his service and of himself which attracted many a worldly Russian. According to Leskov, even the most religiously apathetic person who witnessed Radstock must say to himself that 'he indeed must have true faith; how different from our clergy who function like civil-service men'. Although simple and unassuming, his preaching and Bible reading exercised a great attraction upon his listeners who had never witnessed a religious service other than that of the Orthodox Church. He had come of his own free will without pay, sought no favours of those in power, was earnest and obviously sincere, devoted to his work, defended or attacked no creed; and he lived what he preached. He broke through the established social norms and as an ordinary human being preached the intensity of faith. His direct appeals to his listeners to pray for their own and Russia's salvation left a deep impression on Russian society and caused its members to flock to his meetings."[12]

There were no less than forty aristocratic homes opened to Radstockist meetings. A senior Orthodox priest referred to the St. Petersburg society of the late 1870's, when the movement was at its height: "Not to be a Radstockist meant to lower oneself in the eyes of society and risk the danger of becoming labelled a backward person. To take exception with the teaching of the English Lord in a private home was considered equal to insulting the host."[13]

Chapter 4.
Russia (continued)

The controversy that arose over the movement served to publicise it far and wide. Some considered it likely to develop into a sect and so wanted all meetings banned and Radstock sent home; others, on the other hand, rushed to his defence. Radstock returned in 1875 and 1878 and found that the work was deepening: "Ballrooms were turned into prayer rooms occupied by nobility together with their servants and others of humble origin, by officers, and by university students. Following the example of Radstock many began to act in the name of Christ by aiding the poor spiritually and materially and by petitioning for those who were in difficulty with the authorities. District visiting among the poor in factories, in hospitals, and in prisons was initiated, hospitals and schools were built on country estates, and lodging houses and inexpensive tea-rooms for the poor were established in the capital".[14]

Persecution.

Correspondence not only reveals the widespread character of the movement among the aristocracy but the danger that was being increasingly felt. Count Korff was careful to mention only the initial of his friends, such as Adjutant Baron M. the personal physician of the Emperor, Dr. K. University Professor A. Even Dr. Baedeker, writing to his wife from Russia in 1880, was similarly secretive: "The Princess and Mrs.S, Countess K.'s brother, met me at the station... I dined at Princess M... at 8.30 Bible readings at Princess G.'s... I had a few days with Baron S. and his wife. He is a friend of Princess X". Heier gives an impressive list of the galaxy of names that were known to be followers of Radstock: Madam Chertkova, Count Korff, Princess Lieven and her sister Princess Gagarin, Madam Penker, Col. Pashkov, Countess Ignateva, Count Bobrinsky, Baron Nicolay, Count Shcherbinin, and Madam Zasetskaja, daughter of the famous soldier-poet of the Napoleonic wars, Davydov.

Brobinsky.

Two of those converted through Radstock are worthy of particular attention. Count Bobrinsky was Minister of the Interior. He was of colossal intellect and had read deeply in German philosophy. His soul had found no satisfaction. During the Crimea War, like Radstock, he came to the point of death. He was unconscious for many days. When he came round, his first thought was, "If there is a God, He must have some way of revealing Himself". He then vowed that he would pray every day, without fail, to the God he did not yet know. It was some twenty years later that he met one who had likewise sought his Maker in that same war, but had come into the light of the Gospel.

The contact with Radstock came as a result of a dinner invitation given by Bobrinsky's wife to Radstock. As was his custom, he took the opportunity to bring up the subject of the Gospel, and referred to the letter of Paul to the

Romans. Bobrinsky was half amused and half interested, but could not escape the point. He excused himself and withdrew to seek a way to answer his guest to his own satisfaction. As he went over all his objections, the truth dawned like a sudden flash of light to his soul: "I found that Jesus was the key, the beginning and end of all". Falling on his knees in prayer, he sought mercy and forgiveness and knew straight away that he was forgiven. There was a living God—He had revealed Himself in Jesus Christ. His twenty-year pilgrimage had come to an end.

From that moment in 1874 he devoted his entire life and wealth to the cause of the Gospel, until his death ten years later. His estates became centres of agricultural and social improvement, but first and foremost for the spread of the Gospel. He was eager to witness to his newly-found Saviour, and spent some time to this end with Tolstoy: "It is said that the two men on one occasion spent eight hours on end until six in the morning absorbed in the supreme question of the revelation of God in Christ. The impressions gained after a meeting of this kind are set forth by Tolstoy in a letter to Prince S.S. Urusov dated February 1876: 'Recently I was visited by Bobrinsky, Aleksej Pavlovich. He is a remarkable person, and as if on purpose our conversation turned to religion. He is an ardent believer and his words had the same effect on me as did yours. They provoked an envy of that greatness and peace which you possess'.

A month later, in March of 1876, at the zenith of his religious quest he once more expresses his admiration of Bobrinsky's faith and sincerity in a letter to his aunt, A.A. Tolstaja, lady-in-waiting to the Empress: 'At no time has anyone spoken to me so well about faith than Bobrinsky. He cannot be contradicted, because he does not set out to prove anything; he merely asserts that he believes, and one feels that he is happier than those who do not possess his faith. Moreover, one senses that his happiness of faith cannot be acquired through the intellect but only through a miracle'."[15]

Pashkov.

The most outstanding convert of all was Colonel of the Guard, V.A. Pashkov. He was one of the most popular members of the St. Petersburg society, and among the wealthiest men in Russia. His palace was crowded with treasures. He came to an experience of salvation through Radstock's ministry and opened his palace (now the French Embassy) for regular use in the movement. He had great possessions in the Ural mountains and Central Russia, and used these for the cause. Like Radstock, he would do anything, and speak to anyone for the sake of the Kingdom of God. When Radstock returned to England Pashkov became leader of the movement. This movement was described, in fact, as "Radstockism and Pashkovism" because of the part played by these two men.

Impact on Society.

We can gauge the size of the impact that Radstock had on society in Russia by the treatment the movement received from writers of the time. It was given a thorough handling by better and lesser-known writers who took opposite sides in the affair. Julia Zasetskaja was an ardent follower of Radstock and daughter of a famous poet. She translated "Pilgrim's Progress" into Russian in 1878. Dostoevsky met her and was thus introduced to the movement. He was such an admirer of the Orthodox Church that he found it difficult to see any good in it. Nevertheless, he made some amazing remarks: "It is said that just at this moment Lord Radstock is in St. Petersburg, the same one who some three years ago had been preaching here all winter and also had founded at the time a kind of new sect. At that time I happened to hear him preaching in a certain 'hall' [the American Chapel], and, as I recall, I

Colonel Paschkoff

found nothing special in it; he spoke neither particularly cleverly nor in a particularly dull manner. Yet meanwhile he performs miracles over human hearts; people cling to him; many are astounded: they are looking for the poor, in order, as quickly as possible, to bestow benefits upon them; they are almost ready to give away their fortunes. Perhaps this is so only here in Russia; abroad, it seems, he is not so prominent. However, it is difficult to assert that the full strength of his charm can be attributed to the fact that he is a Lord... It would be desirable that on this occasion no one among our clergy vouch for his preaching. Nonetheless, he does produce extraordinary transformations and inspires in the hearts of his followers magnanimous sentiments".[16] Some were decisively opposed to Radstock and sought to ridicule what was going on. Others were warm supporters. He was insulted and denigrated, and this led to an inevitable reaction.

Tolstoy.

Tolstoy was introduced to the movement by Bobrinsky. He wrote to his aunt: "Do you know Radstock? What impression did he make upon you?" Countess Tolstaja's answer to her nephew in March 1876 was an extensive account of Radstock and his followers in St. Petersburg. Her characterisation of the Englishman, which contains both praise and criticism, seems to be correct: "I have known Radstock quite well for the last three years, and I like him very much because of his extraordinary integrity and sincere love. He is fully devoted to a single cause and follows his path without turning to left or right. The words of Apostle Paul can almost be applied to him. 'I do not wish to know anything but the crucified Christ.' I say 'almost' because in wisdom and thoughtfulness he is not only below Apostle Paul but also below many other less significant teachers of the church".[17] In response, she outlined shortcomings that included what appeared to be a simplistic answer to problems of human depravity and his emphasis on 'sudden' conversion, but added: "But then, what devotion to Christ, what warmth, what immeasurable sincerity! His message resounded here like a bell, and he awakened many who before never thought of Christ and their salvation... Both the praise and the scorn which he received here in St. Petersburg were much too excessive. His public preaching I seldom attended, but I preferred to talk to him alone or in a small circle of friends where I comforted myself in his warm-heartedness and thereby escaped all disputes on dogmatic questions. I think I was one of the few who judged him objectively".[18]

Her objectivity was not copied by Tolstoy. According to Heier, "Tolstoy creates his own image". In his novel, "Anna Karenina", he portrays Radstock under the name "Sir John", and caricatures the religious revival. His own negative attitude comes out clearly when he attempts to discredit the Doctrine of Justification by Faith. He was but reflecting the attitude of those who never understood nor appreciated what Radstock was doing. Tolstoy also introduced Dr. Baedeker into one of his novels. He had been impressed with his work among the prisoners. "He is a Calvinist Pashkovite preacher. He maintained that one ought to preach the Word of God, and that it is not sufficient to shine with good works. I was moved to tears; why, I do not know." Nevertheless, in his novel, "Resurrection", he treats him in a hostile manner. He disapproved of his message, though not of his distribution of the Scriptures, and saw him as a "tool of Providence".

Boborykin was another writer from whose works the widespread character of the movement can be deduced. A reviewer of one of his works stated, "The movement

Dr. Baedeker in Russian attire

spread among the tradesmen and artisans of St. Petersburg, and from there, like a broad wave, it penetrated to various places in our spacious Mother Russia". This was, indeed, the case, and made it abundantly plain that the work was of God and not dependent upon one man.

Radstock's Helpers.

On his second visit to St. Petersburg, Radstock took with him George Muller of Bristol. He was well-known in England for his outstanding work with orphans but was also engaged in regular Christian ministry. He shared with Radstock in the preaching in St. Petersburg. Radstock also introduced Dr. Baedeker to many of the highest social standing. As a result of this, Baedeker obtained the confidence of the authorities and was able to go right across Siberia, visiting the prisons and distributing tens of thousands of Scriptures. This great work occupied him for thirty-two years, in spite of the fact that he had only one lung, a painful curvature of the spine, and a weak heart. As we have said earlier, he was one of the first who was converted through Radstock, and followed his single-minded example.

Pashkov Continues the Work.

It was Pashkov who carried on the work when Radstock left after his first visit, and later, when he was not allowed to return. He declared that he held to the same "Bible Christianity" as that of Lord Radstock. Together with Counts Korff and Bobrinsky, he conducted public meetings. Pashkov was particularly active, using his great wealth in his evangelistic and philanthropic work. He was despised by his fellow-aristocrats, but was tolerated by the Church to begin with. However, his able declaration of the Doctrine of Justification by Faith led inevitably to conflict.

Together with his friends he organised (in 1876) "The Society for the Encouragement of Spiritual and Ethical Reading" in order to make available to the masses the Scriptures and Christian writings. Some of these were prepared by Radstock. This was approved by the Church and the Government. They could see no danger in its publications to begin with, especially as nothing appeared on the surface to be controversial in what was sent out. He opened his home to all, and used his estates in the furtherance of the Gospel, carrying on extensive philanthropic and social work among all classes.

The effect was enormous. When St. Petersburg aristocracy went to their summer residences they carried on their work there. As a result, "Pashkovite nests" were established in nearly every part of European Russia. Peasants in turn spread the Gospel to friends and relations. The message was also spread rapidly by seasonal workers returning home from St. Petersburg with their Russian Bibles and religious tracts. Pashkov and Korff undertook extensive preaching tours into the interior, especially into regions heavily populated by the Nonconformists. The new movement was joining forces with the Nonconformist sects, especially those in the South-West of Russia. But the inevitable happened—the Orthodox Church became alarmed and persecution started.

Persecution.

In 1878, Radstock was expelled from Russia, and public meetings of the Pashkovites were banned. It was, however, harder to deal with the aristocracy than with peasants, and the fires of persecution took some years to be felt. For a number of years the work continued, both religious and philanthropic, with many aristocrats following Pashkov's example. "The Society for the Encouragement of Spiritual and Ethical Reading" continued until 1884, and published more than 200 different pamphlets, some reaching twelve editions. Their total publications reached several million items. The absence of reading matter among the masses meant that Pashkov's work had enormous success. His material (which was free) was almost the only reading available to the people at large.

Pashkov would not be discouraged and, in 1884, sought to unite the scattered evangelical sects by means of a great conference in St. Petersburg. It was a remarkable gathering, but served to alarm the authorities even more, who arrested all the delegates from the provinces. It was now clear that the movement was assuming enormous proportions—they could not stand idly by.

Banishment.

It was reported to the authorities that over 1,500 had been present at Pashkov's palace for worship from every branch of society. Preachers were recruited from among the masses, some of whom almost knew the Bible by heart, it was said. In June, 1884, Pashkov and Korff were both banished from Russia and lived the rest of their days in exile. Heier points out that far more followed Pashkov's example than that of Tolstoy; but few have heard of Pashkov. He practised what he taught, and suffered oblivion; but he sought a heavenly reward and not an earthly… "of whom the world is not worthy".

Pashkov's departure did not stop the work continuing because it did not depend on human leadership. In 1891, a special conference of the Orthodox Church was held in Moscow. Great alarm was expressed at the growth of the Nonconformist sects and Pashkovite "heresies". Twenty-eight out of forty-one dioceses were badly "infected", and persecution began in earnest. The kind of measures adopted then bear striking resemblance to what dissident religious groups have suffered in our day. They were fined, imprisoned and exiled to remoter parts of the Empire. Baedeker met such victims of persecution in his visits to the prisons. Harassment continued, but it did not limit the work, it simply drove it underground.

Survival.

It became impossible for the aristocrats of St. Petersburg to carry on openly as they had done before, but the movement merged with Nonconformity and strengthened the evangelical sects. The Baptists, Stundists (an evangelical sect of German origin), and Pashkovites were treated as one group. There were those in St. Petersburg who still held out. Princess Lieven and other prominent ladies privately defied the authorities by calling prayer meetings and inviting foreign preachers. They also invited preachers from the Stundists and Baptists, which further served to bring the three groups together.

Princess Lieven had supported Radstock, Baedeker and Muller by receiving them as guests and opening her home to meetings. She was reported to the Czar, and was told to stop, with the threat of exile. She responded, "Ask His Majesty whom I have to obey, God or the Emperor". He is supposed to have responded, "She is a widow; leave her in peace". Her daughter, Sophie, visited Mayfield House, Radstock's home near Southampton. An ornamental Russian blotter in the possession of the writer, that had been given to Mr. Payne, one of Radstock's gardeners, is thought to have been given to Radstock himself as a memento from her. Radstock never forgot Russia. He prayed much for the believers there. His last desire was to return, and arrangements were made that he might, in fact, do this; but he was taken home to Glory before it was possible to carry out his plans.

Mayfield c. 1905 by permission of City Museum.

Mayfield c. 1930 by permission of City Museum.

Mayfield c. 1930 by permission of City Museum.

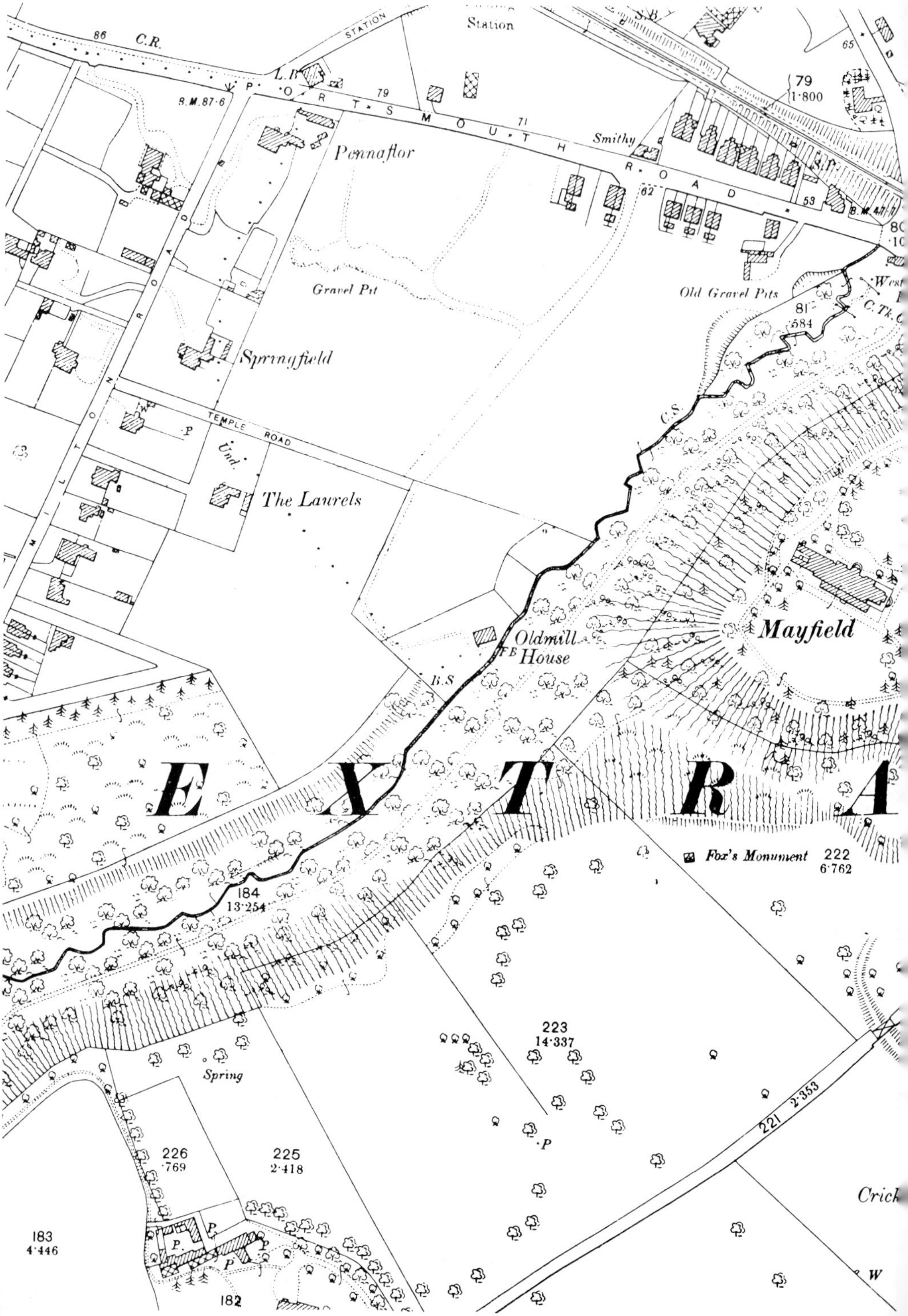
Station
STATION
86
C.R.
L.B
B.M. 87·6
PORTSMOUTH ROAD
79
71
Smithy
S.B.
65
79
1·800
Pennaflor
62
53
B.M. 47·7
Gravel Pit
Old Gravel Pits
81
·584
Springfield
MILTON ROAD
TEMPLE ROAD
Und.
The Laurels
C.S.
Oldmill House
F.B.
B.S
Mayfield
E X T R A
Fox's Monument
222
6·762
184
13·254
223
14·337
Spring
226
·769
225
2·418
221
2·353
183
4·446
182

Mayfield Estate 1897 by permission of City Records Office, Southampton

Southampton Water

15th February 1871.

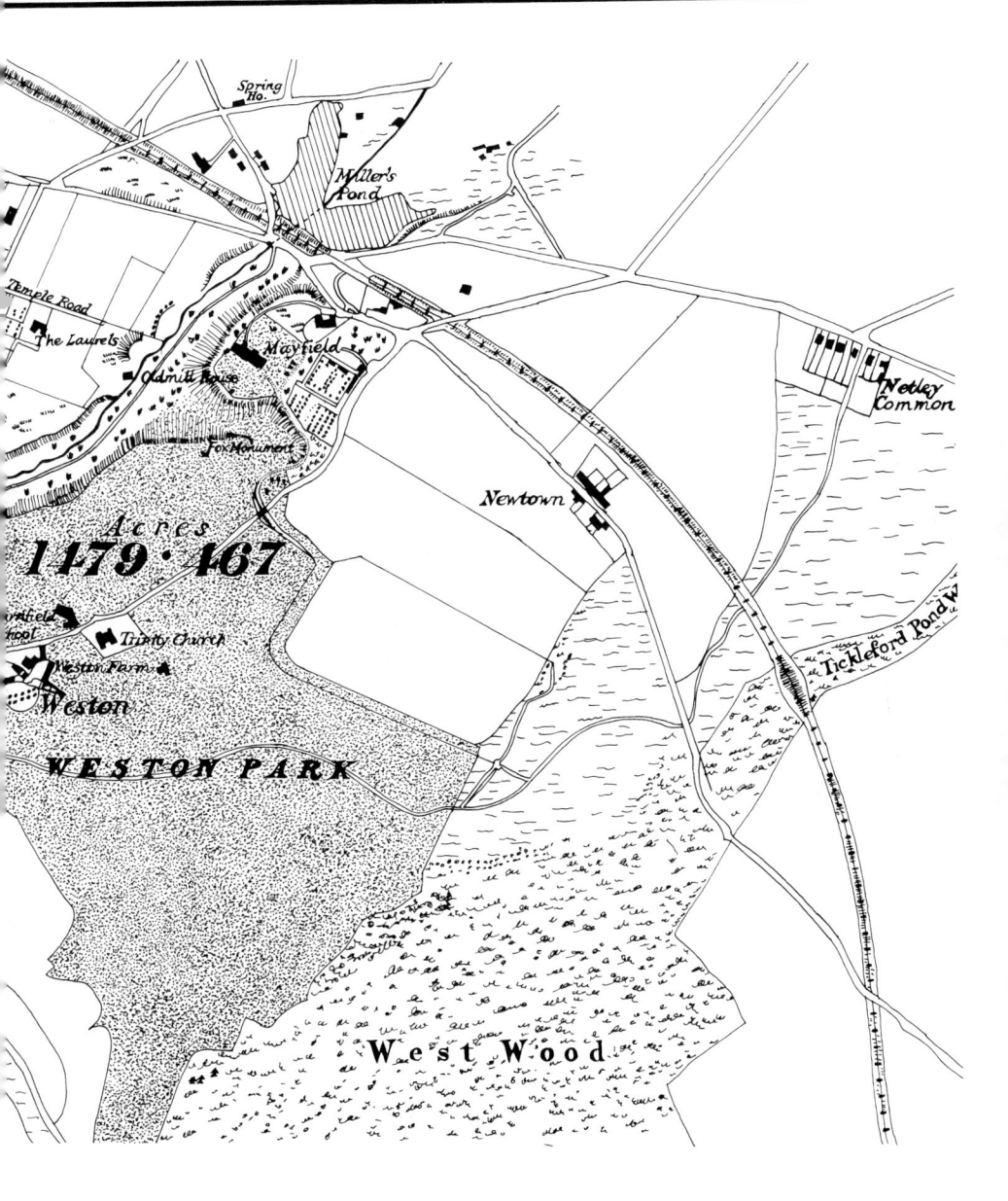

Woolston 1871 by permission of City Records Office, Southampton

Mayfield estate opened as a public park 1938 by permission of Southern Evening Echo.

Radstock Valet John Weller his wife Jean.

Weston Arch upper.

Woolston Weston Arch

Weston Arch lower.

Stables and Lodge as they are today

Russia (continued)   41

Prince Paul   *Prince Anatol*

Princess Mary *Princess Alicia* *Princess Sophie*

Her Highness Princess Lieven and Family

Continuity.

The strength of the spiritual revival in the latter part of the 19th century was such that the work has continued right through the periods of intense persecution to this present day. It became identified as a "Baptist" movement, and its strength and uncompromising testimony are well known today.

Michael Bourdeaux, the Director of Keston College for the Study of Religion and Communism, traces the origin of the Human Rights Movement to the witness of the Reformed Baptists. "In a very real sense the human rights movement of the present day in the Soviet Union originated with a Protestant group, the Evangelical Christians and Baptists."[19] Their unwillingness to compromise with the State for the Gospel's sake has become well known, as have been the sufferings that have been the necessary consequence. It is surely a wonder of our day that such a body has been able to flourish in such a hostile environment. What a testimony to the power of God! It is also a tribute to the one who played such an important role, by God's grace, in its early beginnings. That very commitment and self-sacrifice shown by Lord Radstock a hundred years ago are still seen in Russia today.

Chapter 5.
Further Travels

Sweden.

In the autumn of 1878 Lord Radstock left Russia with his family to return to England, but received a pressing invitation to visit Stockholm. There was a great work of God going on and he was asked to help. He decided, therefore, to return home to England via Sweden and, once there, felt he must remain. The party included Lady Radstock, their seven children, nurses and servants.

The numbers attending the evangelistic services at which he spoke were enormous. He also spoke at Upsala, and his visit was greatly appreciated by the Dean of the University: "I pray God to bless you and all your doings and endeavours for His glorious kingdom, and for the salvation of precious souls. I am sure your joy will be exceeding great in this time and in Heaven". As was so often the case, he had a great influence on the highest in society and among military officers. One example among many will suffice to illustrate the point.

A well-known officer who had just left the Guards was reluctant to make contact with the evangelist, but eventually approached him. He said that, since he was worldly by nature, he felt that he would be quite unable to confess Christ since he would disgrace Him by falling away. Lord Radstock replied by taking out his pencil-case and, holding it upright on the table. He asked Captain A why it did not fall. "Because you hold it", was the answer. "There is then no inherent power in the pencil but a power outside is that which keeps it. God, seeing the utter ruin of man, did not tell him to stand upright, but brought in an external power, Himself. And the question of falling depends not on the power of man, but on the Almighty 'who is able to keep you from falling and to present you faultless before the presence of His glory with exceeding joy'." The message went home. The following year when Radstock visited Stockholm, as the train drew up to the platform, he was greeted by the officer with the words, "God has never let the pencil go for one minute".

The second time Radstock visited Sweden the Chief of Staff opened his house to him and invited all the headquarters staff to attend. He began the meeting himself with a word of personal testimony. Some fourteen years later, one of the officers who had been there told Radstock how he had gone along most unwillingly because all his interests and pleasures had been in the world, but the light entered and he saw Christ as his Saviour. This had changed his whole view of life.

Queen Sophie.

The sympathy and support of Queen Sophie, the Swedish Queen, gave strength and stability to the movement. It is interesting that she belonged to the illustrious house of Nassau, to which William the Silent and William of Orange belonged. She channelled the movement into acts of practical benevolence as well as furthering the declaration of the Gospel of God's grace. By her own people she was regarded as "the Queen of the sick and sad". She had a wonderful testimony. She died within a few days of Lord Radstock, whose friendship she retained throughout her life. The correspondence that they had makes this quite clear.

Skinnarbol, Norway. Konsinnger. 4th Sept.

Dear Lord Radstock,

Many thanks for your kind words of sympathy in my bereavement. I have indeed been in deep waters this summer, but the Lord has sustained me, and I know will sustain me. My dear friend has been enabled by the Lord's grace to be a witness unto Him until the end, and praise Him in the midst of intense suffering. The loss to me is immense, but as you say, in this way we are more and more severed from all ties here below and taught that our Home is above.

    My thoughts are often with you and yours in grateful remembrance of past days.

    Yours in the Lord,   Sophie.

Rosendale 30 May, 1880

Dear Lord Radstock,

Many heartfelt thanks for your kind letter, and words of sympathy, teaching and encouragement. When first I fell ill, I was very desolate, feeling as if God had hid His face; but after a few days, the mists quite cleared away, and I have since then enjoyed such joyful communion with God, and felt His loving presence, more than ever before. Praise be to His name, for His mercy and faithfulness!

It is not Miss Ekatra, but Miss De Geer who is engaged to be married. Miss Ekatra is at present my devoted nurse. I trust that the Lord will always keep her from marrying any who is not a devoted Christian. If you have time and feel inclined, a letter from you will always be much prized by me.

My kindest regards to Lady Radstock.

Ever yours in Christ, Sophie.

Constantinople, 19th April.

Dear Lord Radstock,

As I don't know where a telegram can find you I write these lines to thank you so much for your kind telegram from Brindisi. It did me so much good. My son is convalescent, the Lord be praised! but my faith(less) and thankless heart is still so anxious, and felt very low and lonely in this strange country. That one word: Emmanuel, was just what I wanted. It was from the Lord! It is also such a comfort to know that we have your and dear Lady Radstock's prayers—I was wonderfully helped during the whole journey, the Lord smoothing the way and "making the storm a calm!"...

Pray give my kindest love to Lady Radstock.

Yours in the Lord, Sophie.

Amsterdam, 13th of April, 1882.

My dear Lord Radstock,

I thank you most sincerely for your kind letter, which gave me real pleasure. It interested me greatly something of the mission work going on in Russia, which I trust will prosper and increase. I am confident that the hindrances will at the end only be for a fuller manifestation of the power and glory of God. How one wishes that those in power would understand that the Gospel is their only help! I was so delighted to hear you intend to visit Stockholm. We are there much in want of some refreshing and quickening. I am spending some weeks at Amsterdam to be under the eye of my Doctor, but this time is very precious to me as a time of rest and retirement. I usually live such a busy life of excitement, that I feel it is particularly gracious of the Lord to take me apart for a while. Separation from the world can not and ought not always to be accomplished in an outward sense, but it certainly can and ought to exist in every believer's heart in a spiritual sense. I feel sadly how much I fail in this respect. May our gracious Lord grant me a fuller consecration to do and to suffer His will.

I hope to be at Stockholm in the first half of May; should you return to England before that time, may I hope that your way may take you over Amsterdam. I should regret so very much not seeing you.

Yours in Our Lord, Sophie.

His Preaching.

We get some idea of Radstock's preaching in Sweden from the words of a Swedish officer: "Last Sunday I heard Lord R. preach in Bethlehem Church. I have not till now heard him preach in English without an interpreter, and feared I should not be able to understand him, but my fears soon vanished. His address was, to my mind, masterly, full of life and warmth. He took his subject from Numbers xxiii, where Balak wants Balaam to curse Israel but God forbids him to do so, and commands him to bless.

Instead of the curses that the enemy wished to hurl at the people of God, he had to listen to blessings. What was the reason of this? Had the people of Israel been so obedient and subdued to the Lord that they deserved to be blessed? Had they above everything else loved the Lord who had brought them out of bondage? Ah, no, far from it. Over and over again they had been rebellious against their God... for the sake of the promises given to Jacob, God could not do otherwise than bless his children, for Jacob had found grace with God... But Jacob also required a mediator, a substitute, and he had such a one, and his substitute, his mediator, is a mediator between God and all them who believe on Him. Jesus Christ is The Mediator. If we trust in our Saviour's all-prevailing sacrifice for our sins... God sees them blotted out through the blood of Christ." "This Lord Radstock has something so lovable and peaceful about him. His sermons remind me much of Spurgeon's."

Denmark.

Radstock went on to preach in Denmark in the Spring of 1879. He was on his way back to England with his family but felt it right to conduct meetings in Copenhagen. He had heard about a large Mission Hall that seemed ideal. Before he contacted those concerned, he was approached by the managers of the hall, together with an interpreter! There was great interest, and the hall that seated over 1,000 would be refilled as many as three times in succession. Many of the great were touched, and this had its due effect on society.

Princess Louise, wife of the Crown Prince of Denmark, testifies in a letter to Radstock that it was through his own ministry that she was converted. Her English was good but not perfect. She wrote in 1901, looking back over her life since her conversion, "His grasp, His love, His faithfulness, has not left me through all these 22 years. Just in these days grace penetrated my heart and that you were the man the Lord used, and that you readily follow His will and guidance I never forget. I think it will be of those benefits that we also more shall be able to realise in eternity where many sheaves shall be gathered in by you in which every little straw is precious in the sight of our blessed Lord."

She wrote a number of letters to him and these show the reality of her faith. "Dear Lord Radstock, It has often been my wish to write to you and it increased very much after having received your kind message for me through Miss Ekatra and your dear heartily received letter soon after. It had been my wish to do so because about the time, a little earlier, two years ago, I had the pleasure to see you for the first time and afterward had the advantage to see you regularly during your stay here. No wonder my thoughts often returned to that time. Since then, days have succeeded days, but the Lord in His loving kindness and mercy gave His blessing to the seed then sown so that is enough. His tender care and faithfulness have not been entirely lost but has taken root and perhaps born some fruit. Which it ought to have done but still I must glory and praise the Lord for the change. He, through His Spirit, can change our poor human hearts and let our poor sinful being leap with joy seeing and believing that all has been accomplished on the cross and that we through the blood of Jesus are God's dear children and therefore enjoying the peace that passeth all understanding.

We only can wish that the same blessing may be bestowed on all fellow creatures and one gets quite sad sometimes seeing how little it is understood and appreciated, hardly sought or thought of... How often have I been thinking of my anxiety for so-called pleasures that this winter should bring and how marvelously He has guarded me and held me in His grasp... You asked me to pray for you and I often do but it seemed to me at first as peculiar how much more need I ask you to pray for me. I, such a beginner, am doing so very little for the Lord, and such a coward, quite disgusted with myself, how terrible it would be if we had to do something in order to be saved. Knowing that it is a gift and that this has come there to me through your teaching, what a difference and what happiness... May the Lord's richest blessing be with grace in all your work and all your ways. Believe Me, Yours Affectionately, Louise." More of her letters are included in the Appendix.

As one reads the accounts of many professions of conversion at large evangelistic meetings, the question might well be asked, "Did the converts last?" Radstock asked the question himself in his diary: "Very naturally, after reading these records, someone might ask, 'Did all the conversions last?' Looking back over some fifty years, during which I have seen conversion to God going on, very few have gone back to a godless life, and of these some are known to have been restored through chastening to the joys of the Father's house, while many hundreds are living lives wholly given to God's service". He was strongly against using psychological pressure; neither did he have available the techniques adopted by many modern evangelists to "persuade" his hearers. In his dealings with people he had complete confidence in the ministry and the power of the Holy Spirit to give life. This was borne out by the words of Princess Galitzin. She wrote of her experience of staying with the Radstock family. She was greatly impressed by the example of Lady Radstock, but also spoke of the way in which Lord Radstock dealt with souls. She testified of his discretion and care in the way he spoke to people who confided in him: "He leads them with great ardour to the feet of the Lord but, once there, the servant of the Lord withdraws entirely that the work of the Holy Spirit may be carried on without any human interference".

He travelled to many countries, including Italy, Austria, Switzerland and France, but it was in the more northerly parts that he had the greatest success. We know of outstanding examples of those converted through his ministry, such as Princess Louise and Col. Pashkov, but there must have been many more of humble origin.

Chapter 6.
Southampton and Mayfield

In 1889, Lord and Lady Radstock made the beautiful house at Mayfield their home. It was at that time outside Southampton, in the village of Woolston, (though now that part belongs to the City itself). It had forty rooms, including twenty-three bedrooms. They had ten servants, including gardeners to look after the large 30 acre estate. They had a town house, No.4, Park Square, London, but Mayfield was to remain Radstock's residence until he died twenty-three years later.

Lady Radstock, however, only lived two more years. She was entirely one with her husband in all that he did. She shared the same faith, and was prepared to make the same kind of sacrifices. When he sold his horses and carriage in order to have more to give to the work of missions, she did the same. She also made a very personal sacrifice when she sold her books. Having been devoted to literature, and especially poetry, this meant a great deal, but she felt "called to give up this taste for a more entire devotion".

His Frugality.

At Mayfield he was very careful not to live in style. The late Mrs. Eva McGregor was nursemaid to his grandchildren at Mayfield, then housemaid for ten years. Her observations, made to the author, have been invaluable. She remarked to the writer, "He sold paintings and horses in order to send money to relieve those who suffered from famine in India". On one occasion, going by train, when he was using third-class travel, somebody said to him, "Why do you travel third-class?". He said, "Because there's no fourth-class".

Another eyewitness (who is still alive) is Mrs. Weller, whose late husband was Lord Radstock's valet. She testified to the way he would avoid all extravagance in clothing. "If he could get a tie for 1s.6d., why spend any more?" She told also how he gave away his carriages, all of them, and used a donkey cart. The stables are still there, and are a reminder of his sacrifice. He would urge his servants to avoid all waste. On one occasion he reprimanded them as all the cinders had been thrown away when the fire was remade in the morning, because the large ones could have been used again.

His Generosity.

He was concerned for the poor of the East End and of India, which he visited seven times. On one occasion, when spending a large sum of money for schemes to benefit working girls, a friend found him with a solitary candle and a very small fire in bitterly cold weather. He apologised and said jokingly, "I have enough to eat, but only just. I've not yet come to starvation point".

His Witness.

Many were struck at his level of giving; but he did not give everything away. He kept his house in Mayfield Park, as well as the one in Park Square, London. It meant employing ten servants and he kept beautiful china and silver; but he needed to do that in order to keep in contact with those of his own station in life. He was exercised by the emptiness of London society. He openly declared its religion as hypocritical, its politeness a veneer for jealousy and backbiting, its addiction to entertainment and pleasure a way of escape from conscience. He invited such people to his home in order to witness to them. He saw his special calling to evangelise the nobility. "The Lord seems to send you to some uncommonly pleasant places", someone jokingly remarked at a luncheon party, on a cold November day in London, when he was about to set off for the Riviera. However, Radstock was not seeking warmth, but the frivolous rich. They were unevangelised, dead in sin, sin-sick and desolate, often hiding under a mocking exterior. This explains why he was severe with himself, yet lived in a way that would enable him to maintain links with the nobility. Where he could economise he would—very much so—but where he needed to keep up standards for the sake of his witness, he did so; that was different.

Mayfield House.

He used his home a great deal. Many foreign visitors stayed there, whether princesses or refugees from persecution. He often gave hospitality to missionaries or ministers, to give them a break. One can imagine the benefit his guests would find in relaxing amidst such pleasant surroundings. One of the Czar's daughters, who escaped after the Revolution, and an Indian princess are thought to have been among them. Those who stayed were looked after often by Mrs. Weller's husband, John. One such minister wrote to Radstock to express his gratitude for a few restful days spent in his beautiful Hampshire home. His reply is most instructive: "I am so glad if you got any refreshment while with us. The Lord is always with us. Jacob said, 'The Lord is in this place and I knew it not', but Israel is the dependent one, who cannot wrestle but clings, so he has 'power (1) with God, and (2) with men'. Alas, so often we want to get 'power with men' before we get 'power with God', and we fail."

The estate is particularly beautiful in its undulating character and variety of trees. It is part of the old Weston Grove Estate that was much larger. Two arches used to link the old estate with the grounds on the eastern side of Weston Lane. The upper one had been taken down when the estate was sold in 1938. The lower one survived till 1948.

The Monument.

There is an obelisk on the estate which is now a public park. It was erected in 1810 in memory of James Fox, the politician. It was later dedicated to two horses buried nearby, but Radstock put it to a better use, and inscribed on it the words, "The earth is the Lord's and the fullness thereof", Ps.24:1. The monument could be seen above the trees from his house and was a constant reminder to him of the text. He doubtless chose it with great care. He had much, but it all came from God, and he wanted to give it back to Him. In those days the obelisk could be seen from what is now Obelisk Road, as it is in direct line with it. The obelisk became the trade-mark of Lankester and Crook— a local firm with its headquarters in Obelisk Road. Thus, the obelisk became well-known over a wide area through the firm's twelve branches. It is a fitting memorial to the man who was so utterly dedicated to God.

His Family.

He had three sons. Granville, the eldest, inherited the title but never married.He lived on at Mayfield with his unmarried sisters until he died in 1937. His second son, John, died in 1901 in the Boer War. He had been a barrister at law. His gracious character had endeared him to many. He had considerable talents, and his prospects were good. It was particularly grieving to his father when he died. There is a memorial tablet to him in the local churchyard at Weston, next to the family grave. Radstock's third son, Montague, became the 5th Baron when Granville died. He married and had three children, two girls—Betty and Esther, and a son—John. Montague died in 1953. His son, John, died in the second World War in the navy, so that he never inherited the title. He had married Lady Hersey Goring, and they had two daughters but no son to carry on the title. Mrs. McGregor, who was nurse at Mayfield, remarked how lovely Montague's children were, and added that they would kneel by the settee and pray for their father when he took a meeting.

Besides his three sons Radstock also had four daughters—Edith, Mabel, Constance and Mary. Edith and Mary married. Mabel and Constance devoted much of their time to philanthropic and evangelistic work among the poor and down-and-out in London. They organised soup kitchens, and witnessed to the truth of the Gospel. They would return to Mayfield to rest after their exertions.

Life at Mayfield House.

Lord Radstock used to get up at about 7.00 a.m. and have a cold bath. Then he would pray with his valet, John Weller: "Before we see any other face we must see the Lord's face", he would say. Mrs. McGregor recalled how, each morning between 9.00 and 9.30, Lord Radstock would gather all the family and the servants for morning prayer. Miss Constance would play the piano and his Lordship would give a message. "What stands out about him was his care for his servants. He certainly practised what he preached." At the morning meeting he would pray for each of his servants by name, and pray that all that was done in the house would be to God's glory. His influence, not surprisingly, was very great upon his servants. Mrs. Jean Weller tells how a number of his servants, including her husband, John, were saved through his instrumentality. If, when walking in his estate with a guest, he happened to meet one of his servants, he would introduce him without hesitation as a "brother in the Lord".

Local Evangelism.

Radstock used Mayfield House for regular meetings in the drawing-room. These were held on the Lord's Day and on week nights. He would speak himself, or have a guest preacher. Sometimes he had a series of evangelistic meetings, or a missionary conference. He took a keen interest in the local religious life. When the Salvation Army first came to Itchen village nearby, they were pelted by the crowd, but he stood by them and it was never repeated. He opened their hall in North East Road in 1897.

For a time he attached himself to the Brethren meeting that met at the Oswald Lodge in Woolston. When they built their own "Ebeneezer Hall" in 1901 he gave an

Granville.

Constance.

Family fun.

Lord Radstock with Montague, Family and Friends

Montague.

Granville and Constance.

Lord Radstock with Mabel and Granville

Betty Esther and John.

address. Many of his servants attended, and two of them (the head gardener, Mr. Barfoot, and Mr. Payne) were Elders there. He did not, however, identify himself with any particular denomination. Since he was "evangelical" he was happy to be with the Lord's people whoever they were. He had a close association with the Brethren for much of his life, though the family attended the local Parish Church at Weston. He frequently preached at the nearby village of Sholing, and at Woolston. His nephew became vicar of Sholing (Canon Waldegrave), and his son, Granville, regularly preached at the local Brethren Assembly in Woolston.

Woolston.

Mayfield House itself was not far from Woolston village. Of course, it was far less built-up a hundred years ago, but there were a considerable number of large houses, occupied by the well-to-do who commuted to Southampton. There are still as many as about one hundred such houses in existence, built before 1865. Towards the end of the century, however, there was a building boom following the development of the railway and the Port of Southampton itself, and many smaller dwellings were erected. In 1895, the boundary of the city was extended to include Woolston. Radstock would always walk the mile journey to the Woolston station (before Sholing station was opened), past some of the fine new houses that were fast being completed. We can imagine how picturesque it must have been then; but public health was very poor by comparison, and there was dreadful poverty and sickness.

We have noticed how Radstock was not only a gifted preacher but very good at personal work. A Christian minister gives an example of the way he took opportunities to witness: "On one occasion he was travelling from London to Southampton in a railway compartment, and one of the fellow-passengers was a clergyman friend of his. To my surprise, he entered into an earnest conversation with the clergyman on the subject of conversion, loud enough to be distinctly heard by all in the compartment. In a few moments I noticed the newspapers were lying unread on the passengers' laps, and keen attention was given to the friendly conversation. Then it dawned on me that in this novel but most effective way Radstock was putting before seven or eight passengers the divine plan of salvation. It struck me at the time that the wayfaring man in that compartment, even though unacquainted with spiritual matters, might have gained a clear conception of the way of salvation".

The minister also went to stay at Mayfield, Woolston, and shared a little in a Christian work carried on in a little village nearby. After his wife's death, Radstock gave himself to Christian service with even greater devotion, and spent even more time away from Mayfield.

His Work in London.

In 1884, he started an immigrants' home in London: there were so many coming in from Ireland, Scandinavia, Russia and Germany, and the conditions they faced were terrible. The home accommodated over 600 and, in a few years, 70,000 had passed through its doors. We have already noticed that he was both generous and careful, and there was a story he loved to quote to make his point: "There was an old man of over eighty, whose total income was 5s. a week. One day he brought to a lady visitor 10s. 'I brought this for the poor', he said. Knowing his own poverty she hesitated to take it, but he persisted; and she asked him how he got it.

'You see, ma'am', he replied, 'Everything down here in the East End is a pen'orth—a pen'orth of bread, a pen'orth of herring, and so on. So I buy three farthings' worth instead of a pen'orth, and so I save a farthing; and four farthings make a penny, and twelve pennies make a shilling; and so there are ten shillings.' About six months after, he brought another ten shillings 'for the poor', he said." Lord Radstock adds, "Hath God not chosen the poor of this world, rich in faith and heirs of the kingdom?"

His Example.

While Radstock was doing his work many others were following his example. Fred Charrington, son of the famous brewer, in a tribute after his death, wrote how Radstock had influenced him: "I was Lord Radstock's spiritual godson. It was through him that I was brought into the Christian life and led to give up the trade and great wealth. Indirectly, the Tower Hamlets Mission is one of his works."

He wrote the following in the "Daily Telegraph": "Lord Radstock numbered many distinguished foreigners amongst his visitors, and he was wont to take them to places in London where good work was being done. Our hall had a special attraction, being open night and day, and I have known him bring Ambassadors here. Once his companion was Count Bernstoff, the great friend of the Emperor of Germany, and on another occasion he was accompanied by Prince Oscar, who renounced the Throne of Sweden. A Russian Prince and his sister also came, and they actually helped me in my music-hall work. But his most distinguished companion was the Grand Duchess of Oldenburgh, next claimant to the Throne of Russia, who was accompanied by the Emperor's physician. They were then staying at Marlborough."

He went on to give some interesting information about the support his children gave him.

"The good work of Lord Radstock is being continued by some of his family. His eldest son, the Hon. Granville Waldegrave, is closely following in his footsteps. His sister, the Hon. Elizabeth Waldegrave, has given evening addresses here, and has paid for the erection of a tent in a very poor district. She also works very devotedly amongst fishermen, and I remember her saying at the time of the great revival in Scotland, that when the fishermen came in from the sea, 'Their faces shone with the glory of God upon them'. Further, his youngest daughter, the Hon. Mary Waldegrave, actually came and lived in a house her father took for her right in the middle of the East End, and worked with us until she was married." After such remarks by Fred Charrington, it is not surprising that Mrs. Trotter, who wrote Radstock's biography, should comment, "I found, though, that not the least fruitful part of his life-work lay in the links which he formed between the West End and the East End with its need. He had a peculiar talent for drawing together extremes in society".

Evangelism in London.

He built the Eccleston Hall in London in 1884. He was very much his own man, and his unusual manner of life and outspoken views made it difficult for him to fit into a local church. In the Eccleston Hall he could preach freely. He didn't want it to become a church but a centre where all Christians could meet. He preached there regularly for many years—often to only the coachmen and servants of Belgravia. During the week, however, the hall was filled by various activities,and evangelistic services that drew up to 750. Princess Mary, who later became Queen, often attended these meetings, driving up from White Lodge in all weathers.

Contacts in India.

He spent more time abroad, especially in France and India, which latter country he visited no less than seven times. When he was there he spoke frequently at meetings, engaged in personal evangelism, and sought the well-being of society as a whole. As has been mentioned already, he gave large sums of money for famine relief, but did not leave it there. He sought the help of the British Government to relieve the suffering. He made a request of Lord Salisbury that more might be done for India. The reply was negative but contains a remarkable piece of information that will surprise the historian. In his letter he refers to the reason why we went to war with Russia in the Crimea. Writing from the Foreign Office he stated, "The Crimea War was fought for India, and for India only". It is well known that we were concerned about the threat Russian expansion could pose to India, but it is not generally known that it was for the sake of India alone that we went to war with Russia.

Lord Radstock took a warm interest in the spiritual welfare of Indian students who visited this country. On the death of Queen Victoria, he succeeded in bringing about an extensive distribution of the Scriptures throughout India as a memorial to her. While he was abroad, his home was put to good use. He was anxious to use everything in the service of his Master. After his many labours abroad he must have found it a great pleasure to return to his family and enjoy his grandchildren in the family home at Mayfield; but for Radstock there was no question of retiring. He was soon on his travels again. Not long before he died he had arranged a visit to Russia. Many friends had invited him, and doors were opened. Russia was on his heart to the last. Mayfield House was a delightful place he could return to, but it was only a base for his many activities in his service for His Master.

Chapter 7.
Closing Days

During his last two years, he faced severe physical suffering. On one occasion, when asked how he was, he answered, "I am sent to school". At this time he became acutely conscious of those areas in his life where there was a distinct lack of grace. He thought back to mistakes he had made, and often said, "I begin to see, through God's mercy"[where he had gone wrong]. He was a man of strong views and domineering personality. He could be severe and judgmental, but he was learning precious lessons. He was patient amidst his sufferings, and ready to learn what God was teaching him.

On another occasion, he shared his grief with a lady that few in the upper classes in England would listen to his preaching. This gave her an opportunity to point out how tactless he could be. She referred to some remarks he had made some years previously. She had taken a princess and two ladies with her on one occasion to hear Radstock preach. They were very impressed, and one of them wanted to speak to him, but he had said to them, "You fine ladies are taken up with your lives of pleasure", and this upset her. Radstock was, naturally, very concerned when he heard this, but assured the lady, "Don't worry, you have done me more good than I can say. I thank you from my heart. I am just beginning to learn how great my lack of love and sympathy has been, and I welcome everything that humbles me."

He seems to have learned valuable lessons at this time because, shortly before his death, when speaking at a meeting of the Egypt General Mission, he said, "The Lord Jesus had been taught in suffering, in identification with us, and in order to minister to us He was made perfect through suffering, and because He was a partaker in the suffering He could enter into life in all its darkness. He came into it all, and He says, 'The Lord hath given me the tongue of the taught one that I should know how to speak a word in season to him that is weary'. Jesus had to learn suffering in order to do this. I daresay we all of us at times wonder why this trial has come and that opposition. The Blessed Lord went through that in order to know 'how to speak a word in season to him that is weary'. His whole ministry is sympathetic. It was not as Son of God He came to minister, but as Son of Man… When we have seen this, we shall not shrink from the Cross. Identification with the suffering of the Lord in His service is preparation for ministering."

Closing Days

Anticipating Death.

He had a real sense of the Lord's presence as death drew near. This awareness of the great love of God would, at times, overwhelm him. Not long before he went to be with his Lord and Saviour he anticipated it very keenly. A friend told him of someone who was near to death, and had been given only three months to live. He responded by clapping his hands: "Only think of this, just three months more and then to see the King in all His beauty!" In less than three months it was his own experience.

His Departure.

He kept his hand to the plough to the very end. Three days before his death, he wrote from Paris to a friend, and referred to his eager expectation of the Second Coming of the Lord Jesus Christ. He dwelt on the fact that the Gospel would be preached to all nations before this event, and described what was being done in so many parts of the world. He added, "Here, over four hundred workers received Gospels from me with gratitude in less than seven weeks, only four having refused". Before breakfast, in the cold Paris winter, he left his hotel for this purpose.

He was at the time staying in a second-rate hotel in order to take a series of meetings. He appeared to be in full vigour, but after one of his addresses he felt unwell and was advised to rest. He retired to his small hotel room and his son, Granville, took his place the following evening, 8th December, 1913. On his return, Granville found his father motionless. He had had a heart attack, but showed no signs of a struggle or distress. His wife's Bible was in his hand. He died as he had lived. Luxury was a waste of money that could be better spent for the Kingdom of God. Whilst he was on earth there was much work to do: if unable to preach, he could read the Word of God.

Funeral.

On 13th December, his mortal remains were laid to rest in what was then the country churchyard of Weston Parish Church, near Southampton; it adjoined Radstock's estate. It is now within the City boundary. His body was laid to rest alongside that of his wife, who had died twenty-one years earlier, on the same day of the same month. He was also buried on the same day. The text for the sermon at the funeral service could not have been more appropriate: "For me, to live is Christ, and to die is gain", Philippians 1:21. There was a great company of mourners besides all the family, including a number of working-class people, besides nobility.

Tributes.

Tributes poured in from all quarters. The Archbishop of Canterbury wrote to Montague, his second son, "For more than half a century your father has been in the forefront of work for our Master, and for the advance of His Kingdom, and the whole land is under obligation to one who has rendered such notable service to its highest and most sacred interests". Tributes from a great variety of people struck the same note. His zeal for the Kingdom of God had known no bounds. As "The Times" put it: "Lord Radstock was a man of immense energy and determination, who followed what he considered to be the right path without the slightest regard for the consequences". Radstock would have seen it as simply a question of obeying God's Word.

Memorials.

There is no memorial to this great servant of God on the estate, which is now a public park. However, the lonely obelisk with the text on it from Psalm 24:1, "The earth is the Lord's and the fullness thereof", reminds us of him. Few who notice these words, however, would appreciate how fitting a tribute it is to the faith of the one who put it there. He knew that he had received much and, therefore, much was required, so he gave it all back. There are no male heirs to carry on his title, but he has many spiritual heirs in Russia today, who bear a bright testimony to the faith they received through his labours. The light of the Gospel shines more brightly in Russia today, in some respects, than anywhere else in the world. Such a memorial is most appropriate. That is how he would wish to be remembered.

Personal Witness.

He would speak to anyone of his Master, whether a beggar in the street or a member of a royal family. How many individuals there must have been with whom he spoke of the things of God! The "British Weekly" put it well: "He was never better pleased than when he was expounding the Epistle to the Romans, which he interpreted precisely as Luther interpreted it, and with the same large and liberating effect. He was, indeed, the grand old man of personal dealing". He did not mind what people thought of him; it was what they thought of his Master that mattered. The paper gives us a keen insight into his true humility: "He, himself, was always prone to shrink into the shadow. When asked, as we have often asked him in his latter days, to put into shape for printing some record of his unparalleled experience, the invariable reply was, 'Not unto us, not unto us...'(i.e.'be the glory')... Without profession of asceticism, he lived one of the severest, simplest, and most controlled of Christian lives".

How many there must have been who were not only converted through his words, but challenged by his example, whether a Charrington, a Pashkov, or one of his servants. In his will he left £50,000 net, and included generous sums for his family. He was severe with himself, and generous to the cause of Christ, but he did not neglect his own flesh and blood.

Mayfield House and Estate.

The lovely house near Southampton, in which he lived from 1889-1913, has gone. During the war, it was used as temporary accommodation for the homeless. It became so dilapidated that it was demolished in 1956, just one hundred years after it was built. The beautiful estate, however, has been preserved, but it could have been otherwise. After the death of the 4th Lord Radstock, Granville, in 1937, the estate was going to be sold to W.G. Hinton, a well-known local builder. It was then discovered that, in his will, the 4th Baron required that the estate should be kept as an open space. Mr. Hinton immediately accepted the situation and withdrew his offer. The Corporation then paid the same price for it as Mr. Hinton would have done.

It is now a very well-maintained park, and one of the attractions of East Southampton. Much of the park was already being used for sport, but the whole estate was opened as a public park on 23rd June, 1938. There is nothing at present on the estate to associate the name of Radstock with the beautiful park, though there is a road not far away that bears his name.

His Word to Us.

It is fitting to conclude this chapter with some of Radstock's own words, taken from his notes, so that we can let him speak to us. "Long ago, a poor woman with a very sad history was discussing religious questions with a great Teacher. She was discussing the best form of worship and, like many in the present day, she had her opinions. 'Our fathers', she said, 'worshipped in this mountain', and she herself had the religion in which she was born. Yet some things in her almost wholly darkened conscience did not allow her to rest in the vain conversation received by tradition from her fathers. This made her ready to listen to the tired Man who sat by Jacob's Well. 'You say', she said, 'that Jerusalem is the place where men ought to worship'.

Today, there are multitudes who are arguing as the poor, fallen woman did, with their Lord and Saviour. To them He is saying, 'Neither in this mountain nor yet at Jerusalem shall ye worship... Ye worship ye know not what: we know what we worship: for salvation is of the Jews... God is a Spirit, and they that worship Him must worship Him in spirit and in truth'.

Many are speaking of intellectual difficulties, and inferentially blaming God for an imperfect revelation, while the great Searcher of Hearts would show them that it is sin in their lives, as in the case of that poor woman, which has caused them to wander on the dark mountains, away from that Light that lighteth every man 'by coming into the world'.

But praise Him, 'through the tender mercy of our God, the Dayspring from on High hath visited us, to give light to them that sit in darkness and in the shadow of death, and to guide our feet into the way of peace'. 'This same Jesus', who sought the fallen woman of Samaria, and Saul of Tarsus, a fanatical religionist, is alive still, the Son of Man, 'who came to seek and to save that which was lost'. He, from the Throne of Glory, is still saying, 'Come unto Me all ye that are weary and heavy-laden, and I will give you rest'. 'He that believeth on Me shall not walk in darkness, but shall have the Light of Life'.

For over forty years, these blessed truths have been seen by the writer to be realities. In England, in the United States and India, in Russia, Sweden, Denmark, Germany, France, Italy, Spain, Holland, Belgium, Switzerland and Austria, in almost every conceivable variety of circumstance, in every rank of life, from the highest of all to the lowest, under many varied forms of Christian religion, it has been his great privilege to hear men 'tell in their own tongues the wonderful works of God'.

While many are saying 'What is truth?' and others are groping about and seeking peace, first in one outward form and then in another, the writer feels that he has no longer the right to be silent, and to withhold testimony, imperfect as it is, to the glory of God's Grace. While many are doubting the inspiration of Holy Scripture, multitudes in many lands have, for eighteen hundred years, found by experience that in proportion as they are obedient to the Divine Revelation, not one jot or tittle has failed of the promises of God to those who believe His Word.

By this Gospel some unlearned and ignorant fishermen of Galilee, receiving of His fullness and 'grace upon grace', have become the messengers of the Saviour, so that the Carpenter's Son, as He was supposed to be, is worshipped by tens of millions. His teachings present the most perfect ideals known to the human race, and His Spirit is the one power by which corrupt humanity can be regenerated and changed into the Divine Image from glory to glory."

Appendix.
Letters

The following are letters from Princess Louise of Denmark to Lord Radstock. She married the heir to the throne in 1869. Hans Anderson composed a poem for the occasion. Her husband became King in 1906, so she became Queen then. They are not given in full as parts are missing and the material is not always of especial relevance to our theme. They show again how closely Radstock's converts followed his example. Her English is not always perfect, but her faith is without doubt.

March 24th, 1883.

Dear Lord Radstock,

I was just at the point of writing to you when the post was brought in and with it your kind and dear letter from the 17th inst.

With great sorrow I have heard of the persecutions and the intolerance in Russia, and I feel so grieved at it and even frightened. It is dreadful to have dear and near relations as Emperor and Empress in such a country and now threatening appearing. Everywhere it seems as if the evil grows stronger and more daring but we know that God is the mighty one who can and will save those in the middle of peril who believe in Jesus Christ. What a privilege for those who have been drawn by grace and what a longing there comes in the heart to see souls drawn to the Lord and how we must pity those who reject Him in their blindness and hope others do come to Him.

The other day the Queen took me with her to a hospital. I had taken some text-cards with me and gave to most of them who could read, the only way to communicate with them and certainly they were greedy to get His Word from me. I held them for them to read aloud from the text out of my hand and some looked quite happy and grateful, one who thanked most for it is a man, as I hope, gone home to be eternally with his Heavenly Father.

It is a great encouragement to be allowed so much with Christians, whatever be their denominations and sometimes to be allowed to confess Jesus Christ.

The hall for which you having taken so much interest has been inaugurated. One of these cheering circumstances the Lord sends to those who work.

May the Lord keep, bless and encourage and guide you on your way and in your work is often the prayers of your affectionate and thankful, Louise.

24th June, 1884.

Dear Lord Radstock,

It is only today that I am able to write and thank you most heartily for your last kind letter from Italy. I often wanted to have done so but never succeeded.

A most interesting and blessed time it must have been for you to be allowed to work and see how God in His mercy convinces and opens ways.

I earnestly hope that the work your daughter has taken part in in Italy has proved to be a blessing for many and herself and also has improved her health.

How kindly you rejoice that the Evangelical Alliance is to be at Copenhagen. May God bless those meetings and allow them to be a blessing, comfort and encouragement... It seems many will come. I think most Christians rejoice that it will meet here. Some of the clergy look rather suspiciously on it still. It must mostly be out of ignorance or fear for their own poor influence. But I am confident that the meeting itself will be the best argument against them and show them that they needed not to have been full of anxiety about it.

One thing that perhaps will gratify you, though perhaps you already were told, so that the Queen takes an interest in the Alliance. Several times she spoke to me about it before she left for Germany. I must say I was so astonished... because she joined to it words expressing deep Christian conviction. Perhaps this is now not clear to herself how decidedly she did express herself in the... way to salvation in Jesus Christ and Him crucified, but still my heart hoped with joy that there was a movement for Jesus in her heart. It is answer to prayers and an encouragement to pray more earnestly still for her.

I was ashamed over my astonishment and unbelief in the work of the Holy Spirit and the power of the Lord—you must not think I consider her as a believer yet, no, but I feel confident that the good work once begun shall be wrought out to the glory of the Lord. After the first time she asked me to come again soon after and of her own accord began to speak on the same topic. She has at least no more any opposition to me being a Christian though she still thinks me exaggerated in some points. This is of great notice and a grace of God makings things to look easier. She is an honest one, not afraid to show her conviction. So, once convinced, she will give herself, but there are many old ideas that are to be changed. Often worse for elderly people brought up in so different times. In due time the Lord will bring it out all—He must know much forbearing patience with His children, should He then not have it for those who begin to trust Him and seek Him.

The Crown Prince was asked to patronise the Alliance. He did not accept this and I certainly do see the difficulty in this but promised to be present at meetings. When he told me this I asked him to allow me to go too and take part in them. A desire I did not get but hope it will take place. I pray for this and it is put with God.

The Crown Prince and the children are all well, thanks to God...

My prayer is that He would graciously guide all after His will.

My love to your wife. Often you are remembered in my prayers. The Lord keep us in His grace and in His ways.

I remain always your affectionate,   Louise.

December 31st, 1883.

Dear Lord Radstock,

Before this year comes to a close I must write to you and thank you for all the times you have been praying for me and for the kind dear letters you have written to me.

I am sure if it is God's will you will come and that it will prove to be a benefit and blessing to many. How glad would I be to hear you explain God's own Word again and join spiritually in your prayers.

Concerning my own life, I only can say bless the Lord O my soul and all that is in me bless His holy name. He is faithful, filling me with peace, rest and joy, keeping me near to Him and making my way wonderfully easy. Here and there I am allowed to meet with Christians and they are not quite so afraid to show colours. He has allowed me fully to confess Him several times, and how can I then but praise Him. It is more difficult to rejoice always when it seems as if we are put aside for a time. I suppose it is because it is easier to work for the Lord than to wait on the Lord. This latter makes more training of the Holy Ghost.

I feel uncertain if you are at home though it is safest to address this letter to London.

I must finish my letter. The time has elapsed for this time.

God bless you and all your family, pouring out His grace abundantly and allowing you to draw many souls to Jesus.

If it is God's will I may soon see you, if not there is no distance for God's children. They meet, great and small, at the foot of the cross and their prayers are heard by our Father if we are in Christ.

I remain always your affectionate and thankful,   Louise.

July 10th, 1893.

Dear Lord Radstock,

At length I can write and thank you for your kind letter, it makes me so happy having such a long time since I had any news from you.

Daily I realise what you years ago wrote to me. The Lord is Thy keeper and indeed He is my wonderful faithful gracious keeper.

Jesus still keeps me in communication with Himself, overflowing me with blessings, peace and rest. He who gave His life to save me, this most precious gift should He not give us all we want besides, both patience to bear, love to forbear and thought to conquer. I begin to be more empty and then He can fill and even in His lovingkindness has used me to bring souls to Him.

Only fancy that even this privilege has been granted me. Ah, what a sacrificial blessed Saviour. He saves, He provides, He guides us and we are the apple of His eye. Glorious to belong to Him to render Him grace and homage and to lean on Him. 'He shall do it for His own name's sake' in this is the reliance and the blessedness—not one of His words and promises shall fail. Following close up His footsteps led by His Holy Spirit, we shall prevail.

Palace. January 9th, 1895.

Dear Lord Radstock,

It is so very long since I so very great delight received your letter. I hardly can realise that such a long space of time has passed since I did receive it. The Lord is a precious and faithful keeper and He had been blessing in quite a special way, streams of blessing continually overflow. He has been carrying me on eagle's wings and kept me under His wings.

The other day Countess ... called on me and she asked me to tell you when writing that it seemed to her the time was efficacious for your coming if you had leisure time. Her husband as herself are professing Christians and have a centre for Christian work. She is very interested in all that belongs to the kingdom of God and her drawing-room is always open.

...my boy No.3 is a believer and he says he has given much more than we can long, that is always my comfort as well as praying that His Spirit will keep me ready and vigilant whenever He would so use me in His infinite grace. What a marvel that He who so easily can perform His own work still condescends to have such a poor little fellow-worker as me.

My two dear girls are rejoicing in the Lord. What a grace it is so much easier the more we get gathered together in Christ.

The Queen of Sweden is always weak in health but splendid in spirit. At present we are not going to Stockholm, perhaps later.

The Lord guides us in all after having prepared His salvation. Therefore fear not, the Lord provides and certainly Jesus is never wanting but gives us plenty of His fullness.

Ever I remain, Yours in Christ,   Louise.

June 11th, 1895.

Dear Lord Radstock,

I am so very thankful for your dear letter only it had been impossible to find time and I am not so very strong either, and must take some quiet time daily spent in searching the scripture, otherwise spirit and body do fail. It is the thought of the Lord and His Spirit who sustains me. But then all is well indeed.

Outward difficulties so little and we are in the precious spiritual communication with Jesus, it does pass all understanding and it is a *wonderful blessing daily to live in and on grace. That sweet word which gets sweeter and grander every day*

The Lord provides. He knows but what is best and if difficulties do arise the furnace never gets too hot, for His presence is there and I am wonderfully kept in His arms and oh! how happy and safe in those arms. It is precious to follow the shepherd and know His voice but we the little lambs must be carried. I think it still more a privilege... little ones are faithfully kept. Much is done to drag them away but they are kept in communion with Christ throughout all. Hitherto hath the Lord helped—His arm is not shortened. Sometimes I do fear but then I take my refuge in prayer and leave them altogether to the Lord. He shall take care of them for His own dear name's sake and to the glory of His Heaven so that He once may have them as His jewels in His everlasting crown of glory...

Palace. January 31st, 1898.

Dear Lord Radstock,

The post just brought me your dear letter. Long I have been indebted to you for writing and often wanted to thank, but time is not easily found, still it has pressed on me though it is a small debt in comparison to the great. That one can never be repaid. To belong to Jesus, to rest in Jesus, and sometimes to be allowed to point in Him to others praising a little now and join in everlasting praise before His visible countenance one day will be still better.

The Lord saw that I just wanted an encouragement today and so your letter came... The Lord bless and keep you is the warmest wish of your affectionate and thankful Louise

References.

1. Heier, p.31.
2. " p.32.
3. " p.1.
4. " p.4.
5. " p.21.
6. " p.37.
7. *Men of Purpose* by Peter Masters, p.58.
8. " p.54.
9. " p.54.
10. " p,54-56.
11. Heier, p.45.
12. " p.45,48.
13. " p.52.
14. " p.48.
15. " p.84.
16. " p.61 & 62.
17. " p.84.
18. " p.85.
19. *The Right to Believe*, No.1, 1978.

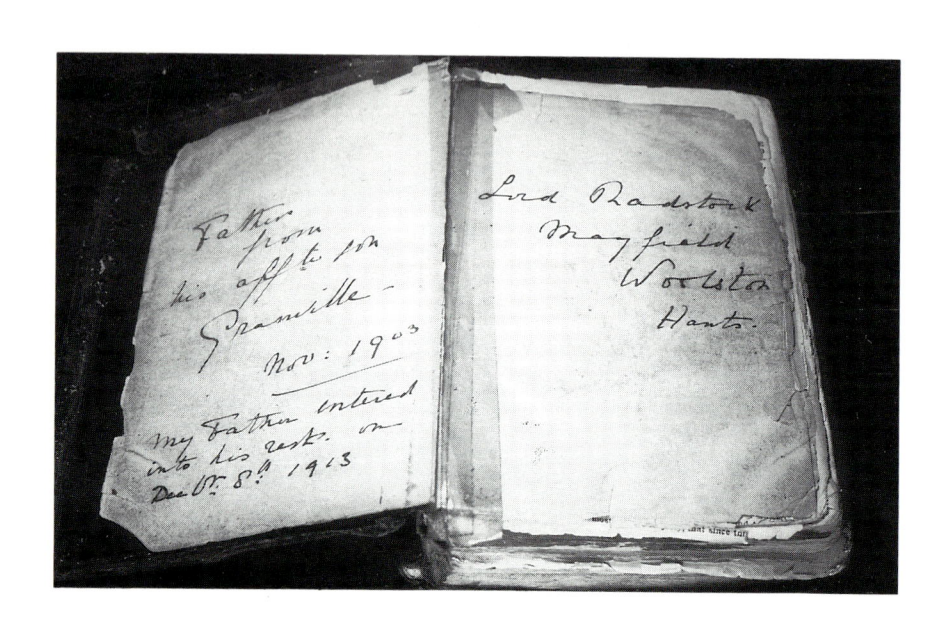

> Father
> from
> his aff te son
> Granville
> Nov: 1903
>
> My Father entered
> into his rest, on
> Dec r 8 th 1913

> Lord Radstock
> Mayfield
> Woolston
> Hants.